PRIMAL ROOTS
SONNY BOND

NUPPERTON BOOKS

PRIMAL ROOTS

SONNY BOND

Copyright © 2016 Sonny Bond

ISBN 978-0-9972932-0-3 Primal Roots Paperback

ISBN 978-0-9972932-1-0 Primal Roots eBook

All rights reserved. No part of this publication may be reproduced, stored in a retrieval system, or transmitted in any form or by any means, electronic, mechanical, recording or otherwise, without the prior written permission of the author.

Published by Nupperton Books, Huntsville, Alabama.

Printed in the United States of America on acid-free paper.

Nupperton Books, 2510 Galahad Drive, Huntsville, AL 35803

First Edition

Table of Contents

Dedication	IX
Acknowledgements	X
Vignettes From a Tall Saddle	1
Model T Time	4
Under The Pomegranate Bush	5
The Day WWII Ended	7
Uncle Stan	9
Little Sister Was Born	11
The Winds of Change	13
Nell	15
A 6 year old Math genius	18
Chores	19
The Boat	21
Waiting for the School Bus	23
Officially Playing Hooky	24
The Privileged Class	26
Building Spree	28
Cow and Train	30
Mount Cristo Rey	32
Up The Hillside	34
The Gold Wristwatch	36
Rattlesnake and Swallows	38
A Memorable Summer	39
Tom and Lulu	43
Raising Chickens	47
Highway Sailing	49
Halloween In the Cottonwood Tree	52
Indian Skeletons	55
Name Calling	58
Forgetting and Remembering	61
Shootout	66

The Mulberry Tree	69
Spiders	71
The Tent	73
Going Camping	76
Desert Fishing	78
Making A Farm	81
Sailboat Races in the Desert	85
Bill's Secret Fort	88
The Farm Bureau Picnic	90
The Mine	92
Riding Calves	94
A Memory of Christmas Magic	95
Guns and Feet	97
Porky's First and Last Ride	100
Reading in the Saddle	102
Boys from the Ranch	104
The Cutting Horse	106
The Dutch Oven	108
The Little Mountain Range	111
TJ	114
Soda Shop Malts	116
Choices	117
College Pigs	120
Insect Collecting	122
A Long Lost Grandfather	124
The Speech	127
College Football	131
Rattlesnake Canyon	135
Leaving Home	136
A New Room	140
The University	143
Pad Sherwood	145
Six Feet Under	148
The Organ Mountains	150
The Volcano	156

Dedication

This work is dedicated to Patti O'Mara who directly motivated me to put down family records and memories in a shareable form. Last Fall, Larry and Patti O'Mara were visiting, and we were talking about our shared family when I mentioned my largely unorganized collection of notes and research material along with my excuses and apologies. Patti looked me straight in the eye and gave me the following order, "Get busy!" This collection of memories literally started being written the day Larry and Patti drove away. Two different journeys began that day.

Acknowledgments

This work was only possible by the encouragement, help and support given freely by my beautiful, creative spouse Vee, and the greatest children any father could have, David, Lisa, and Kaja. Also special thanks to Kaja for her book design and editing, to David for editing and to those friends and family who patiently sat through the reading and re-reading of these pages in progress.

I also want to acknowledge everyone who guided me, shared my adventures and helped me to define the moments of my life. This is a very lengthy list, impossible to make totally inclusive. It begins with those who are mentioned herein but does not end with them. Thank you all for being in my life.

Sonny, Polly and Boopie 1940

Vignettes From a Tall Saddle

Perched high above the ground, I had a good view of Polly's long, pointed ears framed against the sky and desert. Polly's ears were fascinating. They moved, rotated, and twitched while the coarse hair between them flopped around, finally hanging more to one side. My eyes followed the long mane of hair downward until I could see my own small, pudgy, hands holding the saddle horn, then I looked to the right to see the back of Boopie's long, honey blond hair. Boopie was holding Polly's reins as the gentle horse slowly ambled along with me swaying in the saddle. The "clippity-cloppity" sound of Polly's hooves on the sandy ground was hypnotic.

As Boopie turned around to see if I was still holding on, she reassured me, "Hold on Sonny, when we get across the flat, we will turn around, OK." "OK," I repeated. Soon we were headed back toward the house and corral.

"That was a good ride Sonny. You held on like a real cowboy!" she said as she lifted me down in front of her. I followed her to the corral and watched as she took the saddle, blanket and bridle off of Polly and gave her some feed. Then she took my hand and we went back to the house. It was a ritual we shared often, sometimes more than once a day.

At some point, Boopie decided I was old enough to take a short ride by myself. I was perched on Polly's saddle that day in the usual fashion, then Boopie lifted the reins over Polly's head and said, "Now you can ride Polly by yourself across the yard."

Feeling excited and scared, I held the reins tightly trying not to move them. Even though my aunt was not up front with her, Polly plodded slowly across the yard, while Boopie carefully followed our progress. I heard her telling me to pull the reins as Polly and I approached the clothesline on the other side of the yard. I don't remember if I tried to follow her instructions, but if I did, Polly still kept on going. Then I remember Boopie telling me to "Lean over and put your face down!" I could feel the clothesline sliding over me by the time she got there and took hold of Polly's bridle again.

Since the beginning, I called my aunt Ruth "Boop" after "Betty Boop" the animated cartoon character by Max Fleisher about a 1920s Jazz Flapper girl with curly hair that was originally a caricature of Helen Kane, the Vaudeville singer. When I was up there on the saddle, I would call out "Boopie" to get her attention. The name stuck. Everyone called her "Boop or Boopie" for the rest of her life. When I was older, I realized she fit the nickname more than by simply having a passing resemblance to the cartoon.

PRIMAL ROOTS

My aunt Ruth always wanted me to love and interact with horses and other animals the same way she did. Even though I was willing to learn, I was not destined to be her best apprentice in that department. Some years later, her own sons, my cousins John and David came closer to that mark.

Model T Time

There I would be at the round oak table sitting next to my grandfather eating a breakfast of eggs and bacon with toast. Afterward, I would scramble down and follow him as he went into the cellar to get the cool cans of fresh milk and crates of eggs. I stood on the stair landing and watched as he placed all the milk and eggs of the day on the back of his Model T Ford truck. The milk sat in metal cans and the eggs were arranged in racks all tied down on the truck bed. When the load in the truck was ready, he would drive to El Paso and deliver them.

On cold winter mornings, it was always difficult to start the old truck, so my grandfather's solution was to reach down and place one small, crumpled, wad of paper on the ground under the engine, and then with the skill of an Indian scout, surround it with pieces of kindling. Soon it would be ready. I squatted down to examine what he was doing. To me it looked like a tiny campfire.

Usually a single match was enough to light it and after a short time the oil in the crankcase was warmed enough to permit a turn of the hand crank. After a few vigorous cranks, the engine would roar into life and soon Grandfather and his cargo would disappear down the dirt road leading into town. The universe was perfect in my young mind as I grabbed the railing and ran back up the long, straight stairs to see what Grandma was doing in the kitchen and report his departure. Another day had officially begun.

Sonny and Gloria c. 1942

Under The Pomegranate Bush

I know what it feels like to bite into living human flesh. I was standing under the pomegranate bush when this happened. The flesh I was biting was the hand of my cousin Gloria. I don't remember why I was biting her, perhaps she was reaching for the same pomegranate I was trying to pick. Anyway, I was holding her wrist and biting her fingers hard.

Gloria was screaming very loud and the louder she screamed, the harder I bit. Suddenly, I realized our mothers would hear her screams and come outside, so I dropped her hand and ran away. My instinct was to hide. I knew trouble was coming. From my hiding place behind some other bushes, I heard the screen door slam, followed by adult voices of inquiry, "What happened Gloria? Where is Sonny? Let me see your hand."

All this accompanied by Gloria's intermittent sobbing. Then I heard a stern voice begin a sentence with my formal, unfamiliar given name, "Arthur Richard, you come here right now and look at what you did to Gloria!"

I was afraid. Mom hadn't talked to me with that tone of voice before. It didn't seem safe to go to that voice. I stayed put, scrunching lower behind the underbrush and trying to keep real quiet.

Next, I heard my aunt say, "He must be hiding."

"I will find him later, let's go in and put something cold on Gloria's poor little hand," Mom replied.

From my hiding place I then heard footsteps and the screen door opening and closing. What a relief. For the time being I was safe from the posse. However, a four year old can't hide in the wilderness too long. Eventually, I left the safety of the bushes, wondering where to go so I tiptoed around the house toward the screen door stopping when I heard voices inside.

Mom was saying, "Here is some milk Gloria to go with your cookie. That will make your hand feel better soon."

Hearing about milk and cookies was too much to bear, so I opened the screen door and sauntered in as though nothing had happened.

Everyone looked at me and Mom didn't miss a beat. She walked over, grabbed my hand, pulled me over to Gloria and made me look at the awful black and blue bite on Gloria's hand. She said, "Remember, never, never do this again to anyone." Gloria held on to her milk with her good hand and slowly lowered her chubby little swollen hand as I stared at the wound I made.

Then I felt the spanking begin. Soon, I was bawling like Gloria had earlier. It was the first and one of the few spankings I ever got.

The Day WWII Ended

Dad was at work and mom was at home when I went to the neighborhood park to play with my friends. In the ensuing commotion, though, I temporarily forgot all about Mom and Dad.

The park across the street from the apartment where we lived was crowded. I was building roads in the sandbox for my toy cars and trucks when Japan surrendered in August 1945. The streets began to fill with people, and before long I and all the other kids in the playground were surrounded by laughing, hugging, shouting and dancing crowds. I didn't quite know what was happening at first, but they shouted, "The war is over! Japan surrendered! We've won!" Many carried bottles and glasses from which they were drinking, the smell of booze permeating the air. The crowd completely enveloped my friends and I. We simply became part of it. I remember feeling that we should join in and celebrate with everyone else. The fun and the joy was so infectious it became harder to concentrate on my imaginary play, especially when grownups began walking right through the sandbox.

When a tall soldier in his wool uniform offered to boost me up on his shoulders so I could better look around, it seemed like a good idea. At first, it was great fun to see the festivities from that high perch, but things became quickly unsettling. He walked unsteadily, and I began to be able to smell his breath, reeking with whiskey.

I became increasingly desperate to get down as he plodded along in his stupor oblivious to my frantic pleas. "Put me down mister!" I demanded over and over. We were now walking further away from my neighborhood. I didn't know what to do.

Finally, in panic, I kicked my legs free from his grasp and slid down the back of his rough wool uniform to the ground. Free at last, I saw him lumbering away unaware that I was not still riding upon his shoulders.

I turned and ran home as fast as I could, panicked from my scary adventure. This was my introduction to the possibility that joy and good intentions can sometimes go awry.

Uncle Stan

After the war ended, our family finally heard from Uncle Stanford. He was on the Bataan Death March at the beginning of the War and everyone thought he might have died there. As it turned out, he was a prisoner of the Japanese during the entire war. He somehow survived the torture, starvation, disease and brutal work in the prison camps that claimed so many other lives.

One day, in our San Francisco apartment, my dad told me that Uncle Stanford was coming home, and he would be coming to visit us first, before he travelled back to New Mexico. I was so excited, since I had heard so much about him and even though we knew each other before the war, I was too young then to remember that.

My dad was very close to his younger brother and I could tell he also was so relieved and thankful that Stanford was coming home alive. It was like waiting for Christmas, that day. Mom was cooking in the kitchen, making a good supper for all. Dad was trying to wait gracefully, but he would alternately sit, stand, and walk around puttering with this and that. I was arranging some of my favorite toys into adventures when we heard a knock on the door! Dad said "Come in." The door opened and there stood Uncle Stanford, holding a bouquet of flowers wearing his Army Dress Uniform.

He looked at me and called. "Sonny!" I ran to him and he swept me up in the air and then gave me a big long hug. It was such an emotional moment that no one could speak. Finally, he lowered me down and said, "You have really grown-up since I saw you last." Then he and Dad hugged and greeted each other, as only two long lost brothers can, while Mom and I looked on. Then he turned to Mom, hugged her, and remembered the temporarily forgotten flowers he was still holding. Stanford held them out toward her saying, "Margie, these are for you".

Over seven decades later, I still see the room and the open doorway framing Stanford. Then I relive the events and I feel the hug, his thin, muscular toughness, the scratchy wool of his jacket and the smell of his cigarettes. It is that exact moment, frozen in time, when I really and truly knew that the war had ended. That event marked the beginning of my new relationship with my uncle Stanford.

Little Sister Was Born

That October day in 1945 was exciting and very different than any other day in my young life. Dad told me to get dressed, we were taking mom to the hospital because the baby was coming. Soon, we left the apartment in South San Francisco and drove through the hills to the Hospital. I could tell by looking at Mom's face and posture, that something was happening. She wasn't talking much, she looked uncomfortable and sometimes let out a breath and hunched around her protruding belly a little more.

When we parked at the hospital, Mom was taken in and Dad told me I had to wait downstairs in the waiting room until he came back. He said he didn't know how long he would be gone, but I should only stay in that room, because children were not allowed upstairs where he and mom were going. Finally, he said he would come back as soon as he could to let me know how things were going with mom. I wasn't supposed to leave the room unless I had to use the restroom or the water fountain. Both were in the hall nearby. Then Dad left and I began my wait by looking at the magazines in the waiting room. I looked through all the interesting magazines and thought maybe Dad will come back soon.

When he didn't appear, I looked through all the other uninteresting magazines and newspapers. He still didn't come, so I walked around the room and looked out each and every one of the windows. People came and left. A few of them talked to me, and some asked me who I was waiting on. I told them, I was waiting on my dad who was upstairs with my mom.

Finally, I walked out of the room and got a drink of water from the water fountain, then I walked into the men's room, out again and back to the waiting room. I tried to look at some of the magazines again, but that wasn't fun anymore. Finally, I went back into the hall to the water fountain, but I wasn't thirsty so I walked a little further down the hall and then back to the waiting room.

Dad still hadn't come back. I couldn't understand what he and mom were doing up there. I had never waited alone so long in my life. It was very hard to wait without doing something. "I wish I could figure out something to do," I thought. I had already done everything there was to do in and around the waiting room several times. "What else could I do?" I pondered. Sometimes when Dad was at work, Mom would say, "we need to get some fresh air, let's take a walk".

"That's it!" I thought. So I left the room, went out the front door of the hospital and walked all the way around it. "That felt good," I thought as I walked back into the waiting room. I remembered Dad's instructions and felt a little guilty, but I thought, "He didn't know he would be gone this long, so he won't mind if I take a little walk."

I was sure he would come back now after everything I had done, but he didn't. I tried everything in the waiting room over again, and then I took another walk around the hospital building. This time, however, I thought, "maybe if I walk longer, then he will come when I get back." So I crossed the street and walked away from the hospital into the surrounding neighborhood. I walked and walked, looking at all the new sights, stopping to look into shop windows that displayed items of interest to a six year old.

I don't know how long I walked, but finally, I turned around, and retraced my steps back to the waiting room where I climbed up into a chair and started over with one of the much-perused magazines as if I had been perched there all along. Right then my dad, looking tired but happy, came through the waiting room door smiling and said, "Congratulations, you have a little sister!"

The Winds of Change

Like so many other migrant families after the war, my family returned home. We moved back to Southern New Mexico from San Francisco where we lived while dad was working for United Airlines. The Model A was well packed. My baby sister Judy was in between Mom and Dad in the front, and I was perched on a padded platform over the luggage behind them. I had a great view all around and had my books, comics and my tiny die cast fighter planes to occupy me between the outside vistas. Mom and Dad would always tell me about the places we passed, and sometimes we could listen to the radio. Some of my favorites programs were "Judy Canova", "The Lone Ranger" and "Fibber McGee and Molly". Mom and Dad would also tune in some music now and then. "San Antonio Rose" was fascinating to me, especially the original Bob Wills version. All these diversions together with relief stops and diaper changes made the miles and time pass quickly. When we could see the lights of Las Cruces from the crest of the high desert, we knew our destination was near.

Mom's parents, Herman and Martha, lived on the banks of the Rio Grande in an interesting house. Because of occasional river flooding, it was built over a tall stone foundation, which doubled as a cellar. The large upstairs living area was a territorial adobe, with a tin roof and large screened porches front and back. There were two extra bedrooms, which made it possible for us to live with them during our transition.

Mom, Dad and baby sister Judy were in the front bedroom and I was in the back at the corner of the porch. I had my own bedroom in California, so it was a similar situation, but only, until the Spring winds came. That is when the trouble began.

The only heat in the old house was from the sun and the wood stove, and the only cooling was open windows. The windows in my room were fitted with heavy canvas shades, which allowed some air and ventilation, while keeping out much of the windblown dust and sand. However, when the desert winds began to howl, they only added to the overall effect by flapping in and out. The screech owls and coyotes were an added bonus.

It was all too much for my active imagination. I tossed and turned alone in the wind driven symphony until I was frightened out of my mind. I imagined that all the adults and my sister were gone and I was all alone in this spooky old place in the middle of the desert. This went on all night and I just couldn't sleep.

Finally, I got up and quietly tiptoed through the house in the dark, past my grandparent's bedroom, and past my great grandfather's bedroom. When I came to Mom and Dad's bedroom, I quietly tiptoed in until I could see their sleeping forms under the covers and just make out my sister's crib on Mom's side. I don't know how long I stood there, but it was so great to see them, I stood there as long as possible, quietly soaking in all the reassurance that I could.

As I tiptoed back through the house, serenaded by the howling winds, I heard a hearty snore from Great Grandpa Leng's room. That was a present from the Sandman, because after crawling back between my sheets, I immediately fell asleep.

Nell, Boopie, Sonny, Margie

Nell

I was blessed by birth. I was loved and doted upon by my mother and father, both sets of grandparents, nine aunts, seven uncles and several older cousins. All these wonderful people notwithstanding, there is one very special caretaker that must be added to the list.

Her name was Nell. She was very loving and gentle with me and followed me everywhere I went. She always kept a watchful eye on my whereabouts and was ready in an instant to insure my safety, ready to fiercely defend me from any danger I might wander into. I always felt very safe in her presence. Nell was a female German Shepherd.

Nell actually belonged to my Aunt Ruth, my mother's youngest sister. Mothering me was Nell's instinctual behavior. I think she considered me her neediest puppy, one that was especially helpless and constantly requiring supervision.

Therefore, wherever I went, Nell was always there by my side. She watched patiently as I tied a piece of old sheet around my neck, scrambled up a pile of rocks or lumber, then leapt into the air as I became "Superman" for a brief instant. She licked all my skinned knees and elbows until she was sure I was going to be alright. She barked a stern warning at the breeder boar and sows inside the pens as I scrambled up to taunt them. She stood at a respectful distance as I tried to chop kindling by the woodpile, but I am sure she didn't like that.

It was about one third mile through the tangled mesquite dunes above the Rio Grande Bosque from where we lived to my Aunt Effie's house, and I liked to go visit her. Not only was she a very loving aunt, but she also always had a supply of milk and cookies to share when I appeared. This combination was powerful motivation to a youngster like myself, strong enough to cause frequent visits.

Mother allowed me to visit Effie once per day as long as Nell went with me. She trotted along at my side always making sure I didn't stray off course, step on any sidewinders, or wander too close to the river. Usually all it took was a gentle nudge or push from Nell to bring me back to the uncharted sandy path. Only occasionally did she have to get in my face, and vocalize a more persistent warning.

In those days, Nell was my very best friend and constant companion but we spent less time together after I had to start school. The school experience tended to keep me occupied, and Nell, like a good parent, would modify her role to enable her guardians' growing interaction with life.

Once in a while, life can remind someone of what is important in a powerful way. It was a complete shock, something happened to Nell, she was sick, acting strangely, foaming at her mouth. Nell had rabies. I vividly remember the anguished adult faces as my aunt, my grandparents, my mom and dad collectively decided what must be done. I could feel the palpable danger of rabies and serious overtones of our exposure, although I really didn't really understand what it all meant.

It soon became terrifyingly clear as I watched Dad take the rifle from the cabinet, and go out of the house with it. I was horrified as I looked out the window and saw him raise the rifle toward Nell. I closed my eyes for a moment as the trigger was pulled, and I heard the shot. Instantly, my eyes reopened to see Nell slump and fall. A terrible image was burned in my mind forever.

Not a word was said after that, as a giant sadness and mourning gripped our household. Our best friend was gone and the world was suddenly very empty. In a world that often demanded frontier toughness and a stiff upper lip, I suffered her tragic loss inwardly.

In those days, they still gave people the modified Pasteur schedule of Rabies vaccine. For weeks, everyone in our family took daily rabies shots, even my little sister Judy. Life gradually and painfully became a bit brighter. Although we had many wonderful dogs come into our lives after that, Nell always remains in a special place in my heart.

A 6 year old Math Genius

My cousin Florence looked out for me after I started school. She was about six years older than I, so when I was in 1st grade, she was in the 7th. It was a long journey by school bus from where we lived to the little country school we attended. There was plenty of time on the bouncing bus to visit with friends or even finish homework.

One fine morning Florence was doing her math homework, while I, her ever-curious young sidekick looked on. It was very impressive, much more challenging than my simple two number addition. She was working with all the good stuff, like big numbers with three or more digits, subtraction signs, division signs and multiplication signs.

As I watched her, she turned to me and said, "Can you do this? Show me." I dutifully started working the problems with a beginner's enthusiasm. When Florence was satisfied that I was doing them correctly, she let me know it would really help her out if I could finish them. So as the bus rattled on down the road, I eagerly worked her math problems while she continued chatting with her friends. When I completed all of them, she heaped praise upon me until my little first grade head was swollen with pride over doing "big kid math".

I was much older, when one day I realized that I was like the kid white washing a fence for Tom Sawyer. Knowing now what a businesswoman Florence grew up to become, I suspect she may have been selling math homework services to all her friends for a tidy profit!

Chores

Both sides of my family believed in the value of honest, hard work and no one was too young to learn about this. Grandmother (Martha Ellen Reynolds Jundt) did things that were fascinating to me. She would explain that every day we needed wood for cooking and heating and show me how to find the appropriate sizes and qualities of pieces in the woodpile. Then, she would render kindling with the hatchet for starting and stocking the fire. Finally, she would say, "Now, let me see if you can do this." Soon I was bringing bundles of kindling up the stairs into the kitchen and placing them in the bin by the wood stove. It felt good to be able to join in and contribute.

Indeed, my kindly, soft-spoken grandmother, always wearing her bonnet, soon had me drawing half-buckets of water from the cistern under the windmill, and carrying these up into the house through the screen porch into the kitchen. There, the water was poured into kettles, pitchers and basins throughout the house.

Soon I was also tearing rags to fill the rag bags, one for chores and one for the outhouse. I learned which rags were most appropriate for each purpose and how to tear them to the correct sizes. There was even a stack for sneeze rags. Later when facial tissues came along, I remembered that my grandmother already had that function taken care of with a superior product.

My favorite job though, was getting the kerosene lamps ready for the evening. Each day the lamps needed to have the globes polished, the kerosene reservoirs filled, and the wicks trimmed. Working with a table full of fragile glass and brass lamps required the utmost respect and care. To be trusted with this task at my tender age was certainly a rite of passage. To me it was the pinnacle of success, Holy work. I loved everything about it from carefully lifting the sooty globes onto the tray for polishing, to advancing the wicks up for trimming and back down to burning position afterward. The last thing was to remove the cap from the kerosene can spout and precisely pour the kerosene into each lamp reservoir without spilling a drop.

    It was thrilling to be able to report the finished job to my Grandmother. I can still picture her, wearing her apron, bending over the lamps on the table and inspecting each one closely through her spectacles. Finally, she would pronounce the job well done and ready for use. As the last rays of daylight were rapidly fading away, she would tip the globes, light the wicks, adjust the flame and place some of the lamps in the kitchen and dining room. As she did so, my pride glowed as brightly as the lamps did.

The Boat

Boats and water have always been powerful attractions to me. I never knew whether it was because I was born in the desert or if it was in spite of being born in the desert. On my 6th birthday I received some unusual presents. One of them was a boat. Not a toy boat, but a real honest-to-goodness boat. It was a flat-bottomed frame and canvas boat about the same size as a canoe. It had a finely crafted varnished wood frame with varnished wood stringers. A canvas skin was stretched over the stringers and shellacked to smooth perfection. It was made by my uncle Louis and cousin Clarence who somehow decided I might enjoy it more than anyone else at the time. They never told me the reason for the gift, so I am guessing neither of them wanted to use it. Officially, it was from Aunt Lily as well, but I always felt she was involved as a formality.

We were living by the Rio Grande, which did have some water in it during the year. Maybe they thought someone might be able to take me out in the boat. Or perhaps they thought I could simply enjoy it as a play boat. At the time, it really didn't matter to me. I was thrilled. After all how many kids received a real boat for their sixth birthday? I didn't know of any others.

Of course, I begged and pleaded with Mom and Dad to let me sail it in the river but they would not allow it. There wasn't anyone they knew and could trust who had the boating experience to captain the craft and bring their son home safely.

Therefore, I used the boat where it sat in the sand off to the side of the front stair landing. Symbolically, it was sitting by the side of the house facing the river. It was well used in the rivers, streams and seas in my imagination. I would board it hundreds of times. The mooring ropes were cast ashore, paddles dipped into the sand to push the craft away from shore in my imagination. In my mind, the sail was raised and the boat and I went to many distant lands for many fabulous adventures.

In the end, it remained behind like so many things from that time of transition, when my family moved forty miles North and sixty miles West to begin farming. My boat became a treasure mired in the sand and pushed out of my memory for a time by the myriad of distractions which flooded into my experience. On occasion, when it came back into mind, I mused on its fate, and imagined someone finding it buried in the sand, then fixing it up and sailing it down the Rio Grande past the Big Bend to the Gulf of Mexico.

Waiting for the School Bus

When I started school in New Mexico it meant catching the school bus to Canutillo Elementary School several miles away up the Rio Grande Valley. My parents were delighted to have me looked after by my older cousin Florence. She would walk through the sand hills to escort me to school each day.

At sunrise on winter mornings, Florence and I would walk up, carrying our books and lunchboxes, to the sandy rise of a dune by the roadside and wait for the school bus. Since it could be pretty cold, we would stomp down some of the plentiful tumbleweeds on the roadside and she would light them with a match. They would burn quite hot for a short time and we would eagerly warm ourselves front and back. We would repeat the process until we spotted the bus approaching in the distance.

On one particular morning we made our usual tumbleweed fire and huddled in front of it warming our hands, when suddenly we noticed unexpected company. The warm fire thawed out a hibernating rattlesnake that was not at all pleased with such a rude awakening. It was coiled and rattling right behind a smoldering tumbleweed. My cousin and I hastily abandoned that spot and ran to a new location a safe distance down the road. This move, no doubt, allowed the grumpy rattlesnake to focus on moving to a new hibernation spot rather than on us.

Soon afterward, we were rescued by the rickety old school bus which stopped in front of us. Moments later we were seated next to classmates and the rattlesnake was soon forgotten in the dust as we rode off bathed in light from a glorious sunrise to begin another very ordinary day at school.

Officially Playing Hooky

Our school bus in the mid 1940s was an ancient, unreliable thing made before the war and looking suspiciously like a truck that someone simply added some seats and a top onto. Sometimes the engine would overheat and the driver would pull to the side of the road, lift the side hood, pour water on the radiator to cool it down and wait until it was safe to take the cap off and refill it. Sometimes the bus would just sputter and stop running. When this happened, the driver would mutter something under his breath, grab the toolbox and spend necessary time puttering under the hood. On most of these occasions, the bus started again and we went on our way.

There were a few times though, when the bus would simply break down and we would be stranded. On the way home, one winter evening, the bus stopped up on the West mesa. Children who lived at the railroad outpost had just been let off right at sunset, and then the bus broke down near the edge of the mesa as we started our descent back toward the valley and our homes below.

The driver said that someone would find us soon, but it was well after dark when the first headlights appeared. One by one, worried parents appeared in their vehicles to rescue their children and other children who lived near them. On that particular occasion, it was late when I made it home. The day ended on a happy note however. It was too late to be allowed to complete homework before bedtime.

Later, on one fine sunny day, the bus engine caught fire on the way to school. This time, the driver stopped, jumped out and started throwing sand on the engine. He told us kids to all get off and stand far away from the bus. It was exciting to watch as he gradually was able to extinguish the flames and save the bus. Afterward, he turned to us and said, "The bus is broken down, and we are about half way to school. I have to walk back to the district bus yard for help. Each of you all can choose to walk to school or to walk home. Go together, watch out for each other and stay safe."

The choice of the group was unanimous, we all started walking home alongside the river. What a wonderful day as we played, explored, ate our lunches early and had a great time. We all made it home late that afternoon about the same time we would have been let off by the bus anyway. That day we had the best of it all. We played hooky, skipped school, had great adventures and it was all excused and absolutely necessary. We collectively thanked the old, cranky, unreliable school bus for making it all possible.

The Privileged Class

There were few luxuries in the Rio Grande Valley in the mid 1940s, especially in the little, dusty, two-room country school I attended. The teachers were stern nuns, who always carried willow switches to use in place of verbal reminders. The sting of the switch on the back of the hand was quite a motivation to instantly improve one's penmanship. That was the kind of switching I received the most of.

Everything about the school was old. The wooden desks filled with carvings were rubbed dark by use and misuse. The inkwells, which were filled every morning, were stained for several inches around by dripping pen nibs. The worn wooden floor wore a permanent patina of dust ground into it. There were old gas heaters on one side of the classrooms and the only cooling was to open some windows.

The school restroom was an outhouse in the back across the playground field. Only one girl or one boy was allowed to leave the room to visit it at a time. Hopefully, God would help you if someone was out there when you were stricken by an emergency.

School days were long. We kids were out waiting on the school bus before 7:00 in the morning and were returned (hopefully, if the old rickety bus would keep running) around sundown. This was the reality for all children who didn't live within walking distance of the school.

Getting picked up at school by one's parents was such a rare thing that anytime it happened, it was a very big deal, talked about by all the kids for days. A typical schoolyard conversation might go like this:

"Yesterday, Carlos got picked up by his dad at ten right after penmanship and he didn't have to come back the whole rest of the day!"

"Wow!, I wonder why?"

"I think he had to git a tooth pulled out."

"Man, he's lucky!"

It was on a hot Autumn afternoon, that I had my one and only such experience. School had just dismissed and all the children were waiting for the school bus in front of the school. Hot, tired and ready to go home we were holding our bundles of books, lunch boxes and jackets, when we all heard the tinny music of an ice cream truck coming toward us. When it came into sight, it was actually an ice cream motorcycle with a sidecar ice cream cooler. Amazingly, that was the source of the sound!

Slowly, it pulled up in front of the stunned crowd of children, and stopped while the dust was clearing. I immediately recognized the driver in spite of the uniform and special hat he wore. He was my cousin Price! His timing was perfect. He happily sold ice cream bars to everyone able to buy them. Afterward, he motioned for me to climb up and held the cooler lid as I selected from the stacks of frozen treats inside. Then he told me that he was also going to take me home on the motorcycle.

For that one moment, I was king of the mountain, perched on top of the ice cream cooler, eating a Fudgsicle. Then, as everyone in the schoolyard watched with open-mouth envy, the ice cream motorcycle slowly made a U-turn and headed back the way it had come. As it gradually picked up speed, the crowd in front of the school began to recede into the distance. Just before the group of schoolchildren disappeared from view behind the rising cloud of dust, I waved a hand to all in final salute from my perch on the sidecar. I was truly enjoying my brief moment of fame!

Building Spree

There was an old shed, one of many, near my maternal grandparents home. Its sturdy wood frame, was covered with grey, sun-baked boards that were so dry and shrunken that spaces appeared between them here and there. Grandmother had used it over the years for storing items connected with her 'chores'. I rediscovered it when I was almost six years old and looking for a place to make a "fort" as young boys will do.

After opening the creaky door, I entered and stood for a while until my eyes adjusted to the interior lighting. The rays of sunlight beaming through the wall boards here and there created a contrast making it hard to see. "It was perfect," I thought as I ran up the stairs into the kitchen and asked Grandma if I could use it for a fort.

"Why yes," she said, and added, "It could stand to be used again for a good purpose."

I remembered to say, "Thank You!" as I rushed back down the stairs to get busy. After sweeping out the cobwebs and moving a few things, I was soon seeking permission to use some of the piles of scrap wood, old nails, hammer and hand saw.

In my eyes, it was tall enough to easily become a two-story fort. The interior was transformed with a few days of activities including, measuring, sawing, and hammering. I was so proud, the humble exterior of the shed now masked a two-story fort, with four rooms and stairs up to the second level. My comic books and "chemistry laboratory" had been moved in along with a few cloth scrap pads for sitting comfort. It was time for open house.

One-by-one, the adults came to inspect my handiwork, each giving their nod of approval to the remodeling. My grandmother served cookies and milk for the occasion. The fort was a great spot to plan adventures and it soon became "headquarters" for my friends, my cousins and I. Like most things in life, it did have a few flaws, however. The major one was the cracks between most of the wall boards. Because of these it wasn't completely wind proof. Sand storms could easily fill it up with creating sand dunes inside that were miniatures of those outside.

My family moved away when I was nine. I never did return to visit the old place again. Later, it brought a tinge of sadness to hear that my grandparent's land was sold. The buildings were torn down and replaced by new developments. A horse racing track was built on part of the land. All the familiar places were gone. It was as if they never existed. I've learned that the physical world is only part of our reality. The fort is still real in my mind. In a quiet moment, I see myself standing outside my old fort. I see my boy's hand reach for the door, and it scrapes the top of a sand drift as it swings open. I step inside to stay for a little while and watch the sunlight filter through the boards making patterns on my carpentry work...

Cow and Train

Around sundown, a man from Southern Pacific Railroad drove up to our house to let the family know that one of our range cows had wandered onto the track where it was hit by a train. "It needs to be cleared from the track before another train comes through," he said.

After he left, my father, grandfather and uncle were in the kitchen around the old oak table discussing how to salvage the remains of the cow before the next train arrived. Soon my adult male relatives were gathering saws, knives, tubs, buckets, flashlights and lanterns for the task.

I was mesmerized by the proceedings and begged to come along. At first Dad said "no," but I begged and pleaded until he relented. I clamored into the middle of the seat with Dad on one side and Grandfather on the other, while my uncle rode in the truck bed with the gear. We slowly drove through the dark following the washboard ruts that led to the train tracks. Finally, we saw the mangled mound of the poor cow in the headlights and parked in the desert nearby.

As the gear was being unloaded, Dad asked me to hold a flashlight toward the kerosene lanterns so he could see to light them. The lanterns were then placed at strategic points near the remains and the men got to work. My job was to turn on the flashlight and direct some extra light into the shadowy areas as needed.

Before that evening I had only witnessed a few carcasses of smaller animals and some chickens being dispatched, scalded, plucked and cleaned. This however, was a completely different matter. The scale of it was overwhelming. As I stood there in the dark, I was literally surrounded by mounds of warm flesh, blood and organs. The adults were tall enough to rise above the mounds at least part of the time.

I knew that Dad had only let me come after I pleaded and assured him I was old enough to have this experience in a manly fashion and I was determined to hold up my end of the bargain. I was as stoic as possible for a 6 year old, but the heavy smells became more and more overpowering. Finally, I couldn't stand it any longer and blurted out, "Dad, I feel like I might have to throw up!" Dad stopped to focus on my situation. "Come around over here behind me and turn into the wind to breath some fresh air, maybe that will help," he said.

The gulps of fresh air finally did help as I stood and looked away at the star filled sky and not at the mounds bathed in flickering lantern light. Then as I contemplated, returning to my previous assignment, I heard Dad say, "Why don't you go sit in the truck away from the sights and smells for a little while. We can get by without the flashlight for now." I was relieved and eagerly complied with this new assignment.

Sitting that short distance away, I was safe from the immediacy of the sights and smells, so I scanned the sky for meteorites, listened to the yipping of coyotes and peeked over to check the progress as the meat was separated from the rest and placed into the many containers.

I woke up to Dad lifting me over to the middle as he and grandfather climbed into the truck. He said, "We are finished, lets go home, pack all this beef away and get some sleep."

"Dad, I'm sorry." I told him.

"It's OK". He replied, "You learned a lot about life tonight, and this kind of thing is something most of us never get used to. Anyway, we just do what we have to." He started the truck and soon we were bumping away into the night.

Mount Cristo Rey

Mom's youngest sister Boopie was very active, she loved animals and all outdoor activities. She let me ride her horse Polly and took me into the corrals when she tended the cows and pigs. It was always an adventure to follow her around. She told me that the statue of Jesus on Mount Cristo Rey was the same age as I was and tomorrow we would hike up to see it.

She also told me that when she was a young girl, the mountain was named Cerro de los Muleros after the mule drivers who provided the main transportation of goods up and down the Rio Grande since the time of the Conquistadores until trains and autos came along. Sometime in the 1930's a local priest got the idea of putting a cross on the small mountain, which is located on the point of land where New Mexico, Texas and Old Mexico meet. The bishop in El Paso approved, and after a wood cross and an iron one were there briefly, a 29 foot tall marble cross with Jesus was being carved right while I was born. That was such a coincidence that all my life I have felt a special connection to the mountain. It was like my private monument, especially after I hiked up the mountain a few times with my aunt Ruth.

From the trailhead a gravel path wandered a little over two miles around the slopes and rose nearly 900 feet to the statue. We started early in the morning while it was still cool. For the small boy I was, it seemed like a long journey and Ruth made sure that we stopped a few times to drink some water from a canteen. As we gradually climbed up, we could alternately see El Paso, and Juarez. From the North slope we could trace the Rio Grande past the Franklin Mountains up the valley to the Organ Mountains and Las Cruces.

We kept going, discussing the points of the journey and the way the devout pilgrims would kneel and pray along the route. Boopie told me they were reflecting on the journey of Jesus to Calvary as they prayed. Even though I didn't know much about the symbolism, I could feel that somehow we were sharing something from that experience from long ago. Maybe it was also because this desert landscape resembled images of the Holy Land.

When we arrived at the top, there was the statue of Cristo Rey. From where I stood, Jesus seemed so large up on the cross. I imagined he looked at me and knew that I was there. What a fantastic view it was, all I had to do was walk around the base of the statue to see two countries and three states: Chihuahua, Texas and New Mexico.

We rested a bit and started down, which was quick and easy compared to going up. As we walked back home to the adobe by the river below, I would look back to glimpse where we had been. It had been a "Jack in the Beanstalk" experience. We descended from a new world above that was very close to my everyday world below.

For a long time after that, I would look across to the Southeast and gaze at "my mountain". Now the old house and corrals are gone and the community has been renamed from Anapra to Sunland Park, but the mountain I shared with Boopie and Jesus is still there.

Up The Hillside

Growing up when I did, there was a lot of talk about Prohibition and the Great Depression. Different stories were told of how everyone survived these events. I heard how Dad and Uncle Herman went to find work harvesting wheat in the Texas plains and how Mom's family raised and sold meat, milk and eggs. Some of my aunts and uncles had been traveling sales persons. One of the more creative stories however involved my aunt, uncle and cousin up the hillside from my grandparent's house. I would hear bits and pieces discussed by the adults and I tried to figure out what it all meant. It somehow had to do with prohibition, speakeasies and cockfighting. I wasn't quite sure what all this meant, but what I could see was a small ring surrounded by some tiered benches where people came to watch roosters fight. It also had to do with burros laden with tequila and whiskey coming to the border in the dark of night where the booze was passed quickly over the border fence. Apparently at least one grandfather and at least one uncle were involved.

The more I listened, the more interesting and exciting it sounded. There was the Border Patrol trying to intercept the illegal activity of alcohol crossing the border. It kind of sounded like a good game of Hide and Seek at night.

There seemed to be a bit of family pride involved when one of my aunts would state, "The ol' Border Patrol Agent knew they were getting the booze. They found the tracks, but they never could catch them!"

Then another would say, "The agents would stake out every location, but the next delivery was moved to someplace they never dreamed about..."

The conversation went on, "Agent Arnold would tell Mr. Bond when he saw him around, 'We know you're smuggling Mexican booze and we're gonna catch you." But they never could.

'I don't know what you are talking about,' was the only thing Mr. Bond would say."

All this was exciting for a young boy to overhear. It was like Robin Hood and the Sheriff of Nottingham. I wasn't quite sure which one of my relatives was Robin Hood or what happened to the booze they had delivered from Mexico, but I was pretty sure some of it wound up in my Grandfather's pantry. It was also apparent to me that my relatives had developed creative means to endure Prohibition and survive the Great Depression.

I liked to go up the hill and visit Uncle Louis, Aunt Lilly and my older cousin Clarence. When I did, I would look around the place and imagine past times when the cockfighting ring was filled with cigar smoking men brandishing bottles of tequila as the cheered the roosters they bet upon. Then I would feel really proud to be in on the secret, and I always admired Clarence for growing up in the midst of such excitement.

Later, when my uncle and aunt sold their place, it was bought by someone of Italian descent and rumored to be involved with the mob. It became an Italian restaurant and club. I just knew they bought it because of its storied past and that only served to make the family legends more tantalizing to me.

The Gold Wristwatch

My grandfather had the greatest job anyone could possibly have in my six-year-old eyes. To me it was a far better job than being president of the United States. Grandpa was a "Dynamite Man!" His actual job title, I found out later, was "Quarry Foreman." He managed a quarry for a cement manufacturing company. It was his responsibility to drill and set the dynamite charges properly, clear the area for the blast, and afterward to have the limestone ore loaded and transported to the smelter where it was refined into cement.

It was always a treat to visit him in his field office at the edge of the quarry. There was ice water in a big bottle dispenser which one could have in paper cone cups and there was also a real Coca-Cola cooler filled with bottles of various soft drinks. My favorite was the orange soda. Grandpa also kept a basket of Tootsie Rolls on his desk. These temptations, combined with a tour around the quarry escorted by Grandpa created a very exciting visit. The highlight of the tour was the small building which stood all alone that contained the dynamite. My imagination ran wild contemplating the explosive power locked inside it.

Mom and Dad said that soon Grandpa was going to retire and not go to work anymore. That didn't make sense to me at the time. Why would anyone want to stay home instead of going to such a great job everyday? Anyway, it was good to visit him while he was still there.

On one such visit, I got to meet a man that was following grandpa around. Grandpa introduced him and said he was going to take over his job after he left. Grandpa was showing him how to do everything he did. I remember thinking how hard it would be to learn a whole lifetime of work like that.

One day later, we heard and felt a tremendous explosion coming from the direction of the quarry, which was about 3 miles from our house. I heard the grown-ups talking about it. Dad said cars had to go on a long detour to enter the city since boulders blocked the main highway. "It was lucky the explosion didn't injure anyone," I heard them say.

Later, we all rode down to see the area in the family Model "A". I got to ride in the rumble seat. Wow! The power of dynamite was amazing. Boulders bigger than the car were everywhere. One had even smashed the huge steam shovel used to load the ore cars on the railroad. People were talking about how the man who was going to take over the quarry set these dynamite charges during his first day of being in charge. They said that the drill that made the powder holes in the cliff must have hit a crack. The man didn't have enough experience to know how much powder should go into the hole so he just filled it up. It was only when the charge was set-off that the mistake was discovered.

After the mess was all removed, and life returned to normal, the company had a ceremony for my grandpa and gave him a gold wristwatch in a fancy case. I heard that a different person took over his job at the quarry. In my young mind, I was certain that, "the company gave Grandpa a gold watch because they liked him so much they didn't want him to leave."

Rattlesnake and Swallows

The old house by the Rio Grande was home when I came into the world. It was a rambling, rough adobe with a tin roof, built on top of a stone basement. The front and back had rows of pilings under expansive porches. The porches were screened and fitted with long sets of stairs. The stairs in back were angled, with a landing by the windmill cistern from which we drew our water. At the bottom they ended near the wood pile, which was our fuel for cooking and heating. The front stairs were straight and provided an excellent view of the river from every one of the many steps.

One day, my aunt Ruth announced that swallows were building a nest high up on the adobe wall under the roof. After that we would watch their progress every day from outside or by sticking our heads out a window below and looking up. Finally, we could see an occasional little beak open up for the approaching parent bird. We speculated on how long it would be until the fledglings left the nest.

The unthinkable was happening early one morning as I looked up to see a snake clinging to the rough adobe with its head in the nest. I frantically called my aunt for help. She immediately started throwing rocks and clods at the snake, which was about 20 feet above us. One well aimed clod knocked the snake off the nest, and it fell to the ground. Aunt Ruth grabbed a hoe and with one whack beheaded it. Then, she said "maybe some of the birds can be saved" as she slit the snake, removed it's stomach and emptied the contents. I still remember the little slimy forms that tumbled out.

It was a quick and valiant effort, but it was still too late. The poor little things had already suffocated inside the snake. I was shocked and amazed at the great natural drama that just occurred in front of me. Most of all though, I knew I had the most awesome aunt in the entire world.

A Memorable Summer

The man I always knew as my great grandfather, Christopher Leng, as it turned out, was my relative only by marriage. Many years later, I learned he was actually my step-great grandfather. No one ever talked about my actual great grandfather. It was as if he never existed, but that is another story.

I knew Grandpa Leng since birth. He was always around in my earliest memories since he lived with my grandparents, and at times so did Mom, Dad, my little sister Judy, my aunt Ruth and myself. I felt as close to him as I did all the rest of the family. Like my grandfather, he was born in Switzerland and came to America around the same time in the late 1800s.

He had a long bushy mustache, smoked a pipe, and had a heavy German accent. He called me by my earliest nickname Sonny and really rounded out the O as in "SOOOoony" or sometimes he would call me by my other name Arthur. He couldn't pronounce the th sound, so Arthur became "Artoor". My aunt Ruth, was "Rrroot" and he rolled the R as only a German speaker can do.

I loved to visit him in his room. It was different than the rest of the house. I now know it was because the furniture and arrangement was more like the old world he grew up in. I was especially fascinated with his bed stool, his pipe stand, tobacco jar, commode and chamber pot. The whole room smelled like his pipe tobacco.

Since he was a very old man, he walked slowly with a cane. He couldn't hurry down the stairs and go outside to the privy like the rest of the household members did, so his room had a commode with a covered chamber pot inside. When I was a toddler, I also had a chamber pot just like he did, only mine was smaller.

At the dinner table, I often had the place of honor right

between Grandpa Leng and Grandfather Herman. I always wanted to be served exactly the same kind of food they were eating, even if it was liver and sauerkraut. They would take turns passing me things I couldn't reach. Grandpa Leng was always kind, caring and very much a part of my early world.

In the Summer of 1948, my aunt Ruth journeyed to Washington, DC by bus and took me with her. It was the first time since the war that it was becoming easier to get Greyhound tickets for vacation travel. My aunt Kate and her family lived there and no one in the West had seen them since before the war. It had been over seven years. I was very excited to go see my cousins for the first time!

It was a long adventuresome bus ride, which introduced me to places and people I had never known before. Birmingham, Alabama and Chattanooga, Tennessee stand out in my memory, they were so different than anywhere I had been before. The landscape was so lush and green. Aunt Ruth and I arrived in Washington and began a summer that was one long constantly stimulating chain of new experiences. The people, homes, streets, parks, shops, monuments, and everything else were so new and different to me. The way the sidewalks wandered up and down the hills was especially wonderful. "Trikes" and bikes were so much fun there, like being on a roller coaster all the time.

For three months I forgot my little world by the Rio Grande that I had left behind. I was so completely distracted by new faces and places that my prior life became like a distant memory. I was really exited to learn that Aunt Kate and my cousins were going back to New Mexico with us. What fantastic luck!

One day, we all boarded the train to begin that journey. It was my first experience with Pullman car travel. Wow! We rode, slept and ate on the train. My cousin Jerry and I got to share a top bunk.

I suspect Kate and Ruth didn't sleep much on the way back. Supervising adrenaline filled children in a train was like herding monkeys. Whatever was going on out there in the big world around us was of no concern at all.

The thrill and excitement of the summer suddenly changed as my current reality met my past reality. Upon returning, I discovered Grandpa Leng had died! What a shock to me! This was my first direct experience with the concept of human death.

Mom said that Grandpa Leng had fallen down the stairs that fateful morning. He started out with his cane for a morning stroll as usual, and as he started down the long stairway in the front of our house, he fell, coming to a rest in a crumpled heap at the bottom. The others rushed to help and they put him in his bed and went for a Doctor. He never recovered, and died in his bed later that day. I would walk up and down the stair and see all this happening in my imagination. Then I would walk into his room and imagine that part. I felt like some of him was still around. In my mind, I could see him still lying in his bed. When I walked by his pipe on its stand near the washbasin, I could smell his tobacco. It was both spooky and comforting at the same time.

It was so strange, the door to Grandpa Leng's room which he often closed for privacy was now standing open and you didn't have to knock before going in. At first, I would just go in and look around. Later, I would pick up his things and study them, staying in for longer periods. I was fascinated with his pipe, straight razor, razor strop, and felt hat with its satin lining. I made it a daily ritual to go into his room, look around, hold and touch his things and meditate on them. It was comforting and healing to do this. It softened the rawness of it all.

That summer was one of great change. The kind of summer that is forever stamped in memory. It started with travel and adventure, meeting long lost relatives, fun and excitement.

It and ended with loss, and bitter sweet emptiness mixed in. This was an omen, although I didn't know it then, we would soon move away and all that happened in the house by the Rio Grande would become only treasured memories.

L to R: My Sister Judy, Cousins Carol and Gale, Me, Friends Charles, Tom and Tommy

Tom and Lulu

Moving to a new home meant starting all over again with school and friends. When we moved in with my extended family around, I certainly wasn't lonely. Therefore, meeting new friends happened when I started at Lewis Flats School in September. Most of the kids I met lived in and around the same farming community. Among my first new friends were Tom, Charles and Bill. Charles lived half a mile East on the corner of the next farm. Bill lived to the west toward town and somewhat further away. These two friends attended school in the same classroom of the two room schoolhouse as I did.

Tom was in the fifth grade when we met and therefore was in the other classroom. This really didn't matter, since none of the students could socialize during class anyway. Kids could mingle in the schoolyard at recess, lunch, before and after school. Tom lived exactly one-mile West of my house on the same side of the highway. He lived with his aunt Lulu Freeland, who happened to be my schoolteacher in fourth grade.

It was very inspiring to be friends with Tom, who was a year older than I was. Tom was an outgoing kid with many friends and acquaintances of all ages. He also belonged to several clubs and organizations. There always plenty to do when you got together with Tom. He was up on all the latest games and activities.

Tom's aunt was known in school as Mrs. Freeland and she was the best schoolteacher any kid could have. She knew how to help all kids learn while maintaining a great sense of humor. She kept order in the classroom containing grades one through four. She grouped the four grades in different parts of the room and gave each grade work to finish while she instructed another grade. She allowed any student who finished their assignments to silently leave their desk and find a book to read from the bookshelves on the side of the classroom. This was a powerful incentive to learn to focus, complete a task and become a better reader. What I learned in her classroom became a permanent part of my life. Although I knew how to read, I learned to love reading in Mrs. Freeland's fourth grade class.

When you came to visit her home, she always had something good in the freezer or refrigerator for visitors, young and old. What was in her freezer got better the older you became. She always had an ice cream treat for the children, but adults might be offered a frozen "Grasshopper" mixed from cream, creme de mint, and creme de cacao, then neatly placed in the freezer awaiting company.

The fact that your friend's house was right behind the community general store was also very impressive. The store was the only place around where one could buy candy or a soft drink, if one had a little money. A dime in those days could buy a coke and a small candy bar if you returned the coke bottle so there was no deposit.

Lulu and Tom also lived one-mile North of the elementary school. When I rode my bike or walked to school, I could easily stop at Tom's house on the way home. It was a great feeling to get the prior approval needed to stop so I didn't have to go straight home. A good excuse was to ask Tom about how to do homework.

Sometimes, on warm Fall weekends, I would get permission to go to Tom's house and from there we both could walk or ride our bikes to another farm where we visited other friends like Bill or Frank. When we could get three or four friends together, our group would often hike out to the desert ranching country just beyond the Mimbres River basin where most of the farmland was.

Tom's house was also a mile closer to the little Florida Mountains. There we could scramble the slopes, explore old mining camps, abandoned prospector's cabins, and look for geodes of all sizes and agates. There is a canyon on the southeast side known as being a home for countless rattlesnakes. This was also a favorite place for us to warily explore. Tom and I shared many adventures in those days.

Whenever we could we went on our bicycles, although it was common on those dirt roads and shoulders to get flat tires from thorns. Often one would wind up pushing a bike with flat tires as much as ride it Push it at least to the nearest boy's tool shed to fix the flat, and pump the tire again. We all learned how to fix flat tires at an early age. In those days, the hot patch was common, so we really enjoyed clamping the little metal tray with the patch attached to the tire and lighting the material in the tray, which melted the patch rubber onto the tube. That was much more fun than gluing a cold patch on.

Tom and his aunt, whom he always called "Sisso",

broadened my horizons in a number of ways. One was through the National Geographic magazines they always had around. They also let me tag along on many drives into town. Sometimes we visited their friends and acquaintances, which really broadened my otherwise limited social circle. On occasion, I was privileged to accompany them to faraway Silver City to visit Tom's relatives who lived there.

Over the years, the connection to some of my friends slowly faded away. There are a few friends however, who have been present for a lifetime. Tom and Lulu are those kind. He and I have kept in touch since 1948. I also kept in touch with Lulu until she made her transition. Every time I travelled through the area, I made it a point to see her. It was always good to visit with her, catch up on events and share memories while enjoying a frozen grasshopper.

Raising Chickens

My first big responsibility was tending to the needs of a flock of chickens. We would start with a flock of between fifty and one hundred at a time. The chicken coup was completely covered with wire mesh enclosing a small yard picked and scratched clean by the hens. In the middle was a chicken house with a large wooden roost hanging from the rafters by chains.

There were several important tasks involved with the chickens. The first thing was the daily feeding supplement to their foraging diet. Next, it was very important to clean and fill their water containers. Cleaning the coup and chicken house was done frequently. The droppings in yard and in the chicken house were scraped into piles. These piles were shoveled into a wheelbarrow and dumped on a compost pile. Painting all the cracks in the chicken house and roost with creosote was necessary to prevent infestations of mites and insects. Letting the chickens out in the morning was good for their health and really balanced their grain diet with plants and insects. They were especially fond of browsing in the alfalfa pasture amid the cows. Penning them in at sundown kept them reasonably safe from predators like skunks and coyotes. One of the big reasons for raising chickens was, of course, the eggs laid every day.

Gathering eggs was a challenge. Even though we had rows of nests in some of the sheds, they didn't always use them. I had to keep an eye on the hens to find other places they might be laying their eggs. Hens would choose places that were safe and hard to find. A couple of favorite spots were the tops of old tractor seats and under the workbench in the tool shed. You just never knew where they might lay an egg next. It was a game of hide and seek that just kept on playing out.

Most of the chickens at any given time were either hens or pullets. There often was a rooster or two that rounded out the flock. These could be pretty nasty as they are very territorial and don't want anything or anybody close to their flock of hens. Being chased by an angry rooster is no fun for a ten year old boy, but I soon learned to fight back and stay away from those spurs. Most of the time, the adults would slaughter the roosters while they were still edible and not tough as shoe soles.

The one thing that I was not expected to do was to slaughter any chickens. I was spared this responsibility for many years to come. One of my aunts usually did that chore, but sometimes Mom or Dad did it as well. Our family diet featured chicken more than any other type of meat. It was mostly fresh chicken, scalded, plucked and cleaned shortly before it was cooked. I never did like to watch the process, though. When I saw someone carrying a chicken by the legs, I would head the other way. That was also true when I saw the large kettle of water being placed on the stove to heat for scalding.

Aunt Kate's fried chicken was always a favorite at dinner though, especially when served with piles of fresh steamed corn on the cob. After I moved away, sometimes I would go back to visit my cousins and Kate would serve fried chicken. But I never had chicken chores again. Cousin Jerry inherited that job and I heard he was very good at it.

Highway Sailing

In front of the big L-shaped adobe house we lived in was a tall stone fence. A short distance in front of the tall stone fence was U.S. Highway 80. This two lane highway was the southernmost coast-to-coast highway route in the United States at that time. It bisected Luna County, New Mexico, on it's way from San Diego, California to Jacksonville, Florida. Via Highway 80 from our farm, it was around 12 miles West to the county seat of Deming and 58 miles East to Las Cruces.

In those days there was such a small amount of traffic traveling the highway, that we children would ride our bicycles on the highway whenever we could and our parents simply instructed us to get off the road before a car or truck came close. This was an easy thing to do, since any vehicle could be seen or heard for many miles in the desert. The smooth pavement was so much easier to pedal bikes upon than the dirty, rocky, rutted, washboard roads otherwise available. Another huge benefit of riding on the highway was the lack of thorns which flattened tires. We constantly repaired flat tires caused by thorns. Bike tires were simply no match for thorns from mesquite, cactus and goat head vines. We happily pedaled down the highway to reach two very important locations.

The first was West to the little general store. It was only a mile or so from our farm, but it was often against the prevailing westerly winds. This meant it could be hard to pedal when the wind blew strongly, or "kicked-up" as people said. Still, going to the general store was powerful motivation when we had a nickel in our possession for a soft drink or candy bar.

To the East, it was about 12 miles to a trading post, also a tempting destination for 6 to 10 year olds on bikes. There, you could spend your nickel on a Coke and look at Indian artifacts, rattlesnake exhibits and lots of other cool stuff before pedaling back. The only issue was when the wind "kicked-up", it was a very tough 12 mile pedal back, sometimes with sand and dirt pelting you in the face as you hunched over the handle-bars pedaling furiously. This phenomenon was a frequent occurrence. It was a rare outing when there was only a light breeze both directions.

Even though we lived at least seven hundred miles from the ocean, I was always fascinated with boats and sailing. One day, I decided to fasten an old rake handle on the front of my bike like a mast on a sailboat. Then, by adding a broomstick boom some with some old rusty screen door hooks and a sail cut from an old piece of canvas, I transformed my ordinary bike into a sailing bike. To me, it was a magnificent sailing vessel, easily the equivalent of a clipper ship and ready to carry me to exotic parts of the globe.

My cousins and friends pedaled along for the maiden voyage. Wind filled the sail, and soon I was traveling so fast, even without pedaling, that my bike pulled effortlessly ahead of the others even with my feet lifted off the pedals. Naturally, everyone wanted to rig their bicycles in a similar fashion and we set about to complete this transformation. As we hoisted masts and attached booms, we pledged to launch our fleet on a great journey of exploration, sailing at least as far as the trading post.

The next day, our little armada set out in a light breeze, with a few canteens of water and a few snacks. The prevailing Westerly blew us happily onward without pedaling, like conquistadores heading for the new world, content in our immediate success. As we sailed on, the wind "kicked up" a bit pushing us even faster. When we neared the trading post we were doing so well, that we collectively decided it was too soon to end our happy experience. We decided to sail on to the desert highway oasis several more miles eastward down the highway.

As we effortlessly sailed on, the thought of pedaling back started to creep dimly into my consciousness and nag a bit. I brushed this thought aside, returning my focus to the ongoing adventure. We continued until dirt and sand started to pelt our necks from behind. Finally, we stopped, turned around and confronted the enormity of the nearly twenty miles of headwind pedaling needed to get home, all made worse by the now useless, fluttering sail rigging on each bike.

Our mood rapidly changed on the way home as it was very exhausting to pedal against the strong headwinds. We pedaled with sails flapping, and then stopped to furl the sails. Next, we pushed our bikes for a mile or two, finally stopping to rest. Before starting again, we shared the last swallows of water from the canteens. Again growing weary, we stopped and took off the masts with the sails to diminish all the drag possible. After that there was nothing to do except to deal with the sandstorm as best we could, pedaling, pushing and resting alternately. At long last, we made it back, totally exhausted.

After that day, no one ever asked to join me in bike sailing again. Not to be deterred by any minor setbacks, my next brilliant suggestion was bike polo and I will leave that story to your imagination for now.

Halloween In the Cottonwood Tree

  Halloween was a very exciting time even though we were living on farms 12 miles from town. Somehow, my cousins and I were able to improvise costumes and our paper bags were filled with treats as we spooked the adults around the house. Door-to-door trick or treating was only possible if one of our adult relatives would drive us into town and that seldom happened.
  Our Halloween creativity was boundless. In October of 1949, my family was temporarily sharing the large farmhouse with my aunt Kate's and aunt Pat's families situated alongside two-lane Highway 80 in Luna County, New Mexico. Cousin Gale and I had been taking turns on a homemade trapeze we made by climbing up and tying ropes to a large high branch of a big cottonwood tree growing in the front yard of the farmhouse. Even though the tree was behind a rock wall, its limbs jutted far out over the wall toward the highway.
  Gale and I had practiced until we were able to get the trapeze swinging in a high arc further out than the tree limbs extended until the trapeze bar stopped it's arc near the edge of the highway. We would hook our legs on the bar and extend our arms out so we hung there in space for a second before the trapeze pendulum started the return arc.
  It was easy to imagine ourselves, clad in sheets, as ghostly figures sailing out of the tree toward the highway in the dark of a Halloween night in front of an oncoming car. That would surely frighten everyone in the vehicle. Our imaginative young-minds focused on scaring others were not in the least bit concerned with any fear for ourselves.
  So early on Halloween evening, we begged some old threadbare sheets from our mothers, cut eye holes in them and ran around the farm spooking everyone we could. Then, we made sure to garner our share of the Halloween goodies, so our younger siblings wouldn't get them all.

Later, as darkness set in, we began to run out through the open front gate to the highway shoulder to spot any approaching headlights appearing on the crest of the hill which the highway crested a few miles to the West. As soon as we spotted some headlights on the hillcrest, one of us would climb up to the waiting trapeze, pull it back to our launching branch and assume the 'ready to mount and swing out' position. The other would watch the progress of the approaching vehicle, and signal as soon as it seemed to be close enough to spook.

Upon getting the signal, the waiting trapeze artist would swing out of the tree toward the oncoming car, sheet fluttering in the crisp evening air. In our imaginations we were certain that the car would frantically brake, veer to the shoulder and screech to a stop and the passengers would then jump out screaming, "Ghost! Ghost! We saw a ghost!"

In those days, evening traffic on the highway was actually sparse, so it was hard to wait on enough cars to perfect our technique, which we were certain would eventually yield the desired result. Each time, we would improve our timing and strive to get the best streaming sheet ghost effect, until we were quite sure there would soon be panicked passengers frantically, disembarking in front of the farm. Our dogged pursuit of ghostly perfection would yield the imagined results at any moment. Of that, we were quite certain.

Instead, we heard the dreaded voice from the kitchen door in the distance, "Gale, Sonny, it is time to come in and get ready for bed!".

We both yelled back in unison, "Just a little more time ... Pleeeeze!" "Well, OK, just 5 more minutes," came the reply.

The minutes ticked by, and just when it seemed we would have to finally go inside without a good, confirmed ghost haunting, some headlights appeared. As I climbed up to the perch, concentrating on making this a perfect flying ghost appearance, Gale said, "Go!" and I swung out toward the approaching car. It was difficult to see, but I was positive the faces inside looked very frightened, and that the car swerved, just a little. The best part, though, was the honk of the horn as the car continued down the highway into the night.

It was the greatest Halloween night ever!

Indian Skeletons

On a hot summer Sunday afternoon three friends and I had gathered after dinner in the bedroom to figure out what to do the rest of the day. We were all full, completely stuffed as only young boys can be, and casually draped over whatever spot in the room we landed upon. We collectively ruminated over the various possibilities like going up to the mountain to explore or going swimming in one of the farm irrigation reservoirs. Then one of our group said, "Let's get some shovels and go out to the ruins of old Indian village and dig up an Indian skeleton." "Wow! That is a great idea," the rest of us chorused.

Soon, we were all marching up the farm road past the neighboring farm, until we crawled under the last barbed wire fence and went into the dunes of the desert. The remains of the old village was easy to find because of all the pot shards strewn everywhere in the windswept bottom areas between the sagebrush, mesquite and dunes.

We stood there, looking around for likely places to dig. It was a big desert and we never had found anything by digging on other occasions, but young boys are among the greatest of all optimists. Someone would suggest, "how about there?" and then someone else would say, "No, that isn't big enough.. or it doesn't look right!"

Finally, we located a large mound of sand, with a mesquite bush on the far end that we all agreed had "the right look". Then, after subsequent discussion, we decided exactly where to start digging. It wasn't a scientific process, we were "flying by the seat of our pants" using our collective intuition.

We began to dig and there were only empty shovelfuls of sand coming up. What disappointing results. We felt that we were certainly doomed to repeat our previous experiences. The summer sun beat down upon us and it was probably over 100 degrees in the shade. Only there was no shade. We were ready to retreat back to a glass of cool water and to find some shade, when we heard a "clunk" from one shovel!

Excitedly, we threw our shovels down as we knelt and kept digging the soft ground with our bare hands. Gradually, a big pottery bowl appeared. It was colored light grey to white with dark geometric patterns painted around it. A beautiful Mimbreno bowl with one small hole punched through one place in the bottom. The bowl was upside down in the sandy ground. As we hastily freed it from the surrounding ground, I picked it up.

There, underneath it, was the exposed top of a skull! "Holy Cow," one of us exclaimed, "Its an Indian grave! Don't touch it, its bad luck. Let's cover it back up." Before we could start, Charles leaned over and touched one side of the skull. Right before our eyes, the spot crumbled into a powdery pile of bone flakes.

"Damn it Charles, no telling what will happen now, the bowl will be cursed!" exclaimed Tommy. We hastily shoveled sand back on top of the skull, grabbed the bowl and hurried back to Charles' bedroom where we started. We managed to sneak in without any adult seeing us. I shoved the bowl safely under the edge of the bed, but still visible, until we had time to figure out what to do next.

Our collective guilt over removing the bowl from the skull was weighting down the process of deciding the proper thing to do. Now the group must choose something agreeable to all regarding the single treasure item we had uncovered. Hopefully something that would balance the universe again.

We talked for a while, and didn't find any solution, so we decided to wait and try again later. After resting for a time, we started horsing around as boys will do. Charles and Tommy were wrestling and fell over the bed, where a large mill file was perched on the edge. As I watched in horror, the file fell off the bed in the scuffle, bounced and landed squarely on top of the bowl, smashing it into hundreds of pieces! With the smashing sounds all horseplay stopped. The curse of the skull was broken. I went home a bit sadder and wiser. It was a shame, to lose the bowl, but also a big relief.

Name Calling

Children must be reminded by their elders of the ways to be polite and respectful toward others. Actually, they must be reminded quite often. It is literally, the practice of the "Do unto others...." rule. Children do not always understand why we need to behave in this fashion, since they seem to naturally operate at the "Eye for an eye and tooth for a tooth level." One day at school, I painfully learned the truth about all of this.

I was in the fourth grade attending the two-room schoolhouse two miles from where we lived. It was mid morning recess and all the children were active around the schoolyard. Mrs. Freeland and Mrs. Pettigrew, our teachers, were trying to keep an eye on the 50 or so bundles of energy being released after a morning behind the school desks. I was running with some other boys through the crowd when a large girl from a higher grade stepped out in front of me, cutting me off. The rush of anger was immediate, I felt demeaned, insulted, my day was ruined. Couldn't she see the running boys and wait till they passed? Why did she step in front of me? Is it because I'm a scrawny 4th grader? Why? Why? Why? In my flood of negative emotion, I blurted out, "Fatso, can't you see where you are going? I guess you can't because you are too fat....."

She grew red in her face, and tried to slap me. I ducked and ran, still taunting her, calling out more terms of demeanor as I ran. She started chasing me. I ran through the crowd of children playing on the tennis court. Since I thought it would be easy to outrun her, I instinctively wove through the moving group to slow her down even more. I just knew she would stop chasing me when she got tired. By then recess would be over anyway and I would be safely back in the classroom.

All these thoughts and feelings flooded my mind in that flurry filled moment of action. It was all wrong, however. Boy o' boy did I miscalculate. Far from slow, that large girl was actually hot on my heels, and the crowd of people slowed me down, not her. In an instant, she slammed into me from behind, right as I bumped into a couple of people with a basketball, then it ended with a thud, as my face hit the pavement with her full weight squarely on top of me.

    I distinctly remember hearing the crowd rush up to the scene of the accident, as the girl slowly pushed up off my back. It was mostly dark and I felt the moist rawness of my face pressed into the hard pavement at the moment I heard the girl tell the teachers as she pushed up off my head, "He was calling me names." I slowly lifted my head up from the tennis court, where I could see blood and pieces of teeth. My head throbbed and I spit out more blood and pieces of teeth. People helped me inside the schoolhouse and soon, I was lying on my back with a cool damp cloth covering my head. "Lie still until someone comes to pick you up. Mrs. Pettigrew went to find your parents." Mrs. Freeland said.

    My concerned mother and father soon arrived and lifted me into the car and immediately drove straight into town to the Doctors office. After examining me thoroughly, the Doctor said, "He has a concussion, hopefully not too severe. He should rest as much as possible and be under observation. Limit his activity for a week then bring him back for a follow up examination. Notify me immediately if there are any changes. Since his permanent teeth are damaged, he will also need a dental exam as soon as that can be scheduled. We can call the dentist before you leave."

    Mom and Dad were not impressed by my behavior. If I expected sympathy beyond the critical care, there wasn't any to be had. "Serves you right for calling people names. Maybe you will think twice before trying something like that again. When you go back to school, you owe that girl an apology," was all Mom said. Dad looked on in silent agreement.

    It was a lesson dearly learned. The price was paid. In

time my wounds healed, and I did go back to school and apologize. The scars, after effects of the concussion and recurring dental work have served to remind me why the proverbs exist from that moment to this very day. My elementary school literally was the 'school of hard knocks.'

Forgetting and Remembering

It had been a long day at school. Time stands still when a headache begins and you start aching all over. The teachers voice seemed far away and it was difficult to concentrate on what she said to do. I fidgeted and wiggled trying to stay comfortable behind my desk until class was dismissed. With my head pounding and hot it was all I could do to tie my books and lunchbox on my bike rack. Finally, I headed out pedaling, as best I could, down the gravel road to make the two-mile journey home.

It seemed like it took forever. It was a warm afternoon and the more I pedaled, the hotter I became until my head felt like it was on fire. When I finally made it home, I walked in the house to find my mom. As soon as I saw her I announced, "Mom, I don't feel good. I feel sick, my head hurts."

Mom felt my forehead and agreed, "You need to get undressed and get in bed."

I did make it to my bed, but Mom had to help me get my clothes off and lift my legs up on the bed. She took my temperature, looked at the thermometer and said, "You have a fever alright, its 104 degrees!" Then she brought a bowl with some cold water and a washcloth and started putting a cool damp cloth on my forehead.

My teeth were chattering and I was shaking, but the damp cloth did feel good. That was the last thing I remember.

The next thing I saw was Mom's face, still there, smiling at me. She was still wiping my forehead with a damp cloth. "Welcome back! Your fever broke!" she said.

I was confused. "Back?" I asked.

"You have been mostly unconscious for four days. The Doctor said you have a severe case of measles," she said.

"The Doctor?" I whispered.

"He came out here from town to examine you, when you

were delirious with fever. I don't think you knew he was here."

I saw Dad come through the door behind Mom. He walked over with a big smile to greet me, "Welcome home son! It's good to see you looking like yourself again. You gave us quite a scare for a few days." Then he added, "Rest up and get your strength back, and I'll be around to check on you after lunch."

Meanwhile, Mom brought me a little clear broth in a cup and propped me up with pillows so I could sip on it. My mind was full of questions. "Mom," I said, "Where do we go when we are unconscious?"

"I don't know," she replied, "Maybe just off to dreamland, or maybe nowhere at all."

"Why can't I remember where I was for such a long time?" I continued.

"Maybe you will later. Memories have to rise up from below our consciousness. Anyone can suddenly remember something they didn't know they forgot anytime. Perhaps it's a little like bubbles rising up through water," she speculated.

"Yeah," I agreed, "When the bubble bursts, then that's a memory!"

"Indeed," Mom said, "Now try to drink some more broth."

As I lay there sipping on the broth while pondering what Mom said, I began to feel very relaxed. Soon another memory bubble was formed as I drifted back to sleep.

After a few days, my appetite and strength returned and life went back to the way it was before the measles. I was blissfully unaware that it wouldn't remain that way very long at all.

I was back in school for only a few days, when something strange happened. I was told later that I suddenly fell over and went into convulsions. The teacher and students were surprised and horrified that something like that could happen so unexpectedly. When I woke up, I couldn't remember anything, even who I was or where I was. Some woman and man who looked familiar were standing over me, talking to me. Then, the man carried me out to the car and placed me on the back seat. They said they were taking me to the doctor. I felt terrible. My head was, throbbing intensely, my tongue was too painful to move, I was bruised and ached all over. Even the light hurt when I opened my eyes. I just lay there bouncing on the back seat listening to those people in the front talking and kept my eyes closed with a cloth over my face. The darkness was soothing.

The doctor examined me and said he was going to prescribe some medication to try and prevent this kind of thing happening again. I was horrified to hear that it might happen again. Then the three of us got back into the car and left. By now, I had learned these people were my parents, but honestly, I couldn't remember them, they just seemed familiar and kind. After sleeping the rest of the day, my memory seemed to be gradually returning and then it happened again.

The next few weeks were pure Hell. Luckily, my memories from this time are very spotty at best. The seizures were so frequent that I experienced several a day. My parents told me about it all later. I realized my family and I had become hostages to the condition I was experiencing. Our peaceful rural life was totally disrupted by constant trips to specialists, laboratories and hospitals near and far. During this time, it was impossible for me to attend school. The best that could be arranged was for me to try to do my assignments at home when and if I was able to focus on it. Because I was experiencing such frequent loss of consciousness and amnesia, dealing with daily homework assignments was essentially impossible.

The few recollections I have of this 'lost period' of my life include being told what happened by different people and not remembering any of it. I became a confused and passive recipient of the news. The world of my larger exuberant experiences had quickly become very small, fragmented, and random. Much later I realized that most people go through their days assuming their identity is permanent and continuous. I learned not to make this assumption when I was still a boy.

Around 1950 medical treatment for neurological disorders was much less available than today. Many doctors tried to help my situation, but it took a long time just to see if any kind of medication would change anything. While all this was going on, I was prodded, poked, x-rayed, and x-rayed again and more. Everything was explored that medical technology could offer to do in those days.

Depending on which way you looked at it, the high and or low point in my clinical testing came when one neurologist decided to pump air into my spinal column to obtain a clear x-ray of my spinal cord. It was done under general anesthesia, so I didn't understand what they had done until I came out of the anesthesia into the most intense pain possible.

It was total pain throughout my entire body, constant and excruciating. It was impossible to lie still, or to move. Nothing I did would lessen it one bit. No position offered relief, no up, no down, no painkillers, no nothing. The constant excruciating pain lasted for days. I couldn't sleep. I couldn't stand to be awake. I wanted out of my body and I was having an in-body experience with a spinal cord that was being squeezed along its entire length. I rolled back and forth across the hospital bed, stood up on the floor, got back in bed, stood up on the bed, lay down, shook my arms and legs, shook my head, lifted my head and legs and arms, and any combination of the above.

I kept moving like this for two days, until I was a totally exhausted heap of protoplasm, but still in pain in my entire body. Eventually, slowly, the air began to find its way out the tissues and the pain gradually subsided. All other pain I have experienced in life, thus far, pales by comparison. I know now the difference between total pain and throbbing pain. Throbbing pain, when it occurs, is a blessing. Throbs grant us tiny pulsating retreats from pain that makes it more bearable. Total steady pain takes the experience to another level.

Within a few years, the frequency of the attacks diminished. No one knew if it was spontaneous or because of medication. Some of the doctors thought the condition was triggered by either the concussion or the severe case of measles, which both occurred shortly before the onset. I was determined to live a normal life and not let the condition define me. My parents were absolutely the best parents I could have had through the entire ordeal. With their help and understanding, I was able to move past the worst times and continue living as a functional person.

The scariest part of the whole experience was the amnesia that came after every episode. Sometimes memories returned sooner, but after the more severe events, it could take several days. It is a very uncomfortable disconnected feeling. I became expert in pretending I could remember something until I actually could. Somehow that seemed to make it easier to interact with others and continue on with life. If there is an upside, it is that I learned that I could survive even this level of chaos in my life.

The only way I can describe the feeling is like waking up in a total sleep fog with a huge headache and not having it clear up. I became aware that identity is a gift. It is truly temporary and can go away in an instant. Whoever we really are is still there even without identity. Later in my life, the episodes went completely away as if they never occurred. I can testify that miracles can happen and prayers can be answered. It just might take a while.

Shootout

Bows and arrows were a favorite activity for boys in our Luna County farming community where I lived. Inspired by reading and re-reading Howard Pyle's 'Robin Hood,' I made several bows during those early years. I was constantly experimenting with new kinds of wood, though one of my favorites was the local yucca stem. Whenever I found a large, straight yucca stem, I would take my pocket knife and carve it into a bow. I would begin by leaving a suitable round section in the middle for a handle grip and then shape one side at a time into a flattened flexible limb of the bow. I used the strongest twine I could find, twisted it double, bound loops on the end and waxed it to make a bowstring. I made scores of bows and actually became semi-proficient at it. Proficient enough to show and help my friends also make bows.

Over time, I was finally able to buy a bow from the hardware store in town. To be honest, a commercial bow made from good quality wood did shoot better than most of my homemade bows, but it was still fun to make them.

Arrows on the other hand, were very hard to make, although I tried many times. It was difficult to find any round, straight material for shafts. Also it was difficult to find, cut and fasten straight sections of feathers onto the shaft and notch a shaft without destroying the end. There was nothing easy about arrows. Bows were always a simpler item to construct. Arrows were a constant problem to both shoot and retain in good condition. They were always breaking, and getting lost. I did learn to take parts from broken arrows and use them to repair damaged ones.

My cousin Jerry and I and most of our friends had bows and arrows. We would hold archery contests shooting into bales of hay for hours at a time. One nice thing about living on a farm was that hay bales for targets were relatively easy to come by.

We would go hunting with bows and arrows, although it was very rare for any of us to actually hit anything. Most of the time we wound up target shooting at different objects we saw in the desert.

    One particular day, Jerry and I went into the desert to the North of a neighbor's farm. It was an area we were pretty familiar with and the closest place where there had been an old Indian village centuries before. We actually would find pottery shards, and beads, on a regular basis. On occasion we would also find an arrowhead or two. We left our bikes at the end of the road near a barbed wire fence which separated the farm from the range country to the North. Things were kind of quiet, and after walking around for a while, we stopped to shoot some arrows at a few rusty cans.

    Finally, we headed back toward the place we left our bicycles. Along the way, I challenged Jerry to see who could shoot an arrow the farthest. Each of us selected an arrow, nocked it on the bowstring and drew back until the arrow tip was just past the bow grip. We angled our arrows upward for maximum ballistic effect. One after the other, the arrows were released. Both went high into the air and then we lost sight of them.

    As we walked along we scanned the desert floor and the flora for arrows sticking up in the ground at a high angle. Finally, we spotted one and walked over to retrieve it. It happened to be Jerry's arrow and it was fairly near the fence were we crossed over earlier. We hadn't seen any sign of my arrow. Taking one last scan 360 degrees around the area, we still had no luck. I did a quick double back a hundred yards or so to look again, even walking to the sides of where I imagined it would be. No trace of my arrow was seen. Thinking it was lost, we crossed the barbed wire and went to pick up our bicycles. Suddenly we both spotted my arrow, it was sticking up from one of Jerry's bike tires, which obviously was quite flat.

What a letdown for Jerry, he had been thinking he had won the shootout, only to find my arrow in his tire a few yards further on. To put it mildly he was mightily upset with the situation. I knew he was pissed at me when I tried to apologize and he would not answer. He picked up his bike in stoney silence and started pushing it down the road, looking straight ahead. I followed along for a while pleading with him to ride my bike home and I would push his instead. I did feel bad about the outcome.

Jerry was locked into his fate, he kept walking steadily along ignoring me and my pleas as if they had not been heard. Finally, I gave up and wobbled along slowly peddling nearby. We covered the mile back home this way. There was no way I could gloat over the small victory. That day, we both were equally robbed of victory, and each of us learned that sometimes winning and losing can be the same thing. There is no way to predict this possible outcome, I realized. Eventually, Jerry settled back into his usual good natured, full of heck self. I warily avoided any suggestion of bow and arrow shootouts for quite a long time.

The Mulberry Tree

There was a large Mulberry tree growing on my uncle's farm within walking distance from our house. More than "just a tree", it was a lofty world separate from the everyday one below. Each summer, it would produce thousands of large, luscious, berries. The adults would occasionally nibble on one plucked from a low hanging branch, but we children knew how to feast upon them. All it took was basic tree climbing skill. There was no particular age when this might be obtained. It was an individual ability that simply appeared. Both skill and opportunity came together when luscious berries were hanging above the heads of agile children. It was still impossible for the very young, who would simply stand under the tree, reaching longingly toward the berries, until finally they would resign themselves to await their future turn and leave.

It was obvious that the adults had lost their tree climbing skills somewhere along the way. A future without tree climbing, did not trouble us in those days. It seemed so very far away. It was indeed a rite of middle childhood to be active, agile, balanced and coordinated enough to grab a branch and ascend the tree like any self respecting Gibbon.

My cousins, friends and I would spend hours climbing up into the shady branches where we could stand or sit while picking and eating the deep purple berries. We stood or sat on strategic branches where the canopy could be scanned for the proper dark colored berries. The berries too pale or too red were left to ripen. Only the proper deep hued ones were plucked and savored. Like monkeys, we literally lived in that tree for days. Cousin Gale, slim and agile, was a full-fledged member of the monkey tribe. She could scramble further out than anyone in search of the most perfect jumbo berries.

Of course, our clothes became stained and streaked with mulberry juice. We were quite a sight at the end of a day in the tree. Our farmer parents never worried much about how we dressed or looked. They knew the importance of a fully involved childhood and what that entailed. One modern convenience they did appreciate, I noticed, was a good washing machine. Of course, a basket or bowl full of ripe mulberries delivered daily by a 'monkey child' was kind of a nice convenience also.

Spiders

Each year in the spring tarantulas would hatch out and walk around the desert doing what tarantulas do. They are fascinating creatures, spiders large enough to have a demonstrable personality. In spite of their fierce looks, they are actually fairly docile, and will even tolerate being picked up and handled carefully.

If there had been enough Spring rain, the spider hatching could be large and there could be a migration of thousands of tarantulas, enough to see lots of squashed tarantula bodies on the roads where some would invariably be run over. I remember just such a year.

Judy and I were visiting our cousins Jerry, Mattie, and Mary. At some point on each visit we also would see Cousins Carol and Gale, who lived a short distance away across the highway. Often, the whole group would gather together at one place or the other. We had driven up from the south of the county. Jerry and I were out in the yard studying wayward tarantulas that walked through the gate into the driveway and we also went out to see the remains of the unlucky ones on the road.

We were bending over and examining the spiders who would often stop for a moment and look at us, with eight eyes, as if they were returning the examination. Being a little wary, I will say respectful, of spiders myself I was content to let Jerry pick them up. It was enough to have performed the boy's tarantula rite in front of my peers some years earlier. To become a full member of desert boyhood, one needed to pick up a tarantula, set it on their arm and let it walk up at least to the shoulders. Better yet, letting it walk until it came down the other arm was considered very macho. Having performed it once, there was no way I felt any need to continue the custom.

In the middle of our tarantula examinations that day, we

were reflecting on how frightened some of the girls were acting when they saw a tarantula. Maybe we could casually put one in the house, we thought. Then we could casually hang out in another room until we heard the screams. On second thought, it didn't seem to be such a good idea. What if the tarantula hid somewhere and it was Aunt Kate or Uncle Bob that discovered it? We had to think of something different.

I can't remember the way it was discussed, but we came up with a great way to surprise the girls with a tarantula. In the end, we tied a thread around the waist of one large spider and hung it, eye level from the door frame to the girls room. We could hear their voices around the corner, inside the room as we pushed in the thumbtack with the thread and spider attached. Then, we hurried, silently down the hall into the living room and waited.

The expectations were building as we pretended to be occupied with magazines sitting there in the living room. Just when we wondered if the spider was still hanging there and almost ready to go back and check, we heard the screams! Then, we did what all perpetrators of such crimes do. We doubled up with laughter while the troupe of furious girls marched past us, glaring accusingly at us, on their way to tell our parents.

The Tent

It was a beautiful autumn day, a perfect day for camping in the yard and to let childhood imaginations run where they will. Jerry and I had decided to use a fifty-foot cotton trailer tarpaulin to make a tent. It took a while to figure out where to put it. We had never engineered a tent with poles and stakes alone. Our only previous experience had been to stretch a rope between two trees in the forest or between two pre-existing supports like telephone poles or any solid uprights that were tall enough. We decided to stick to our tried and true method.

This time we were lucky and found two small trees in the side yard, between the house and the stone wall which surrounded the yard. The trees were exactly the right distance apart. A strong rope was stretched between them as high as we could put it. It was just high enough to hold the heavy tarp without swaying too far down in the middle.

It was tent to be proud of and large enough to pique the imagination toward palatial grandeur. We started planning rooms, with furnishings and all the livable touches. Of course, all this work and planning required frequent snack breaks especially while searching for tent improvements.

Our parents informed us that they were all going to a farmers meeting in town for the afternoon and asked that we look out for the place and each other. They were giving us the responsibility to be on our own for several hours, and we assured them we were up to the task. They left and the feeling of absolute power enveloped us. We took blankets from the house and hung them up to make rooms. Next, we used any stools, spare chairs, cushions, small shelves, tables, and more to enhance our comfortable desert nomad style decor.

Many trips were made as we became more and more creative with our chosen spaces. Of course, we had frequent show and update sessions to remain abreast of the latest developments in each interior space. Finally it was time to luxuriate in our newly appointed environments. We transferred many treasures like stacks of comic books next to blanketed lounging areas. That made it possible to kick back with a tall glass of cola and a comic book, which we did to celebrate our days work. All of our younger siblings came to inspect the handiwork and hang out for a while, running back and forth in and out.

By then, the shadows were growing progressively longer, the sun was beginning to set, and the air began to develop a significant nip. This required some careful thought. It was obvious that a little heat and a few flashlights would provide light and comfort through the evening until our parents returned and we were called in at bedtime.

"No problem," we thought as we looked at the way the Indians heated their teepees and decided it would work for us too. In the middle of the tent the patchy grass was cleared from a space and a small wood fire built there. We were very careful to make it small and keep it away from any hanging blankets. Since there were open ends on the tent, we figured that would be plenty of ventilation. It worked! One tiny little fire made it so cozy in there. It was perfect!

Only one small chore remained before we settled in, that was to get food for our supper. A short trip inside to the kitchen to make sandwiches took care of that. As we walked back around the corner of the house holding our plates full of tasty sandwiches, we were horrified! Our tent with all its contents were gone and the trees were charred black. Nothing was left, except small piles of burning, smoldering embers surrounded by a ring of burning grass.

We ran up and stomped the grass fire to keep it from spreading and during the action, managed to remember the garden hose to spray water over the area. Finally, we managed to extinguish all visible signs of fire, even spraying up into the trees and every spot that emitted a tiny curl of smoke.

The burned area was on the side of the house, so it was barely visible from the driveway or the entrance. One actually had to walk around to see the full extent of the damage. It was all hidden by darkness after the sun went down. That was when all the adults returned from town.

They came home to find a group of casual, quiet children as if it had been the most ordinary of afternoons for all. That, in itself was probably very suspicious. Of course, after a few questions were asked about the quality of our activities, the truth began to tumble out until we finally made a full confession.

The judgement was that I, being the oldest, should have known better than to do something completely stupid like starting a fire in the tent, and further that we all had learned a valuable lesson in putting out fires. Since we were still alive and well and only objects had been sacrificed, they were thankful and we should be also.

We were also told to be grateful that the house hadn't caught fire and we still had a roof over our heads. It was definitely a "Go forth and sin no more" evening. One to lie awake and ponder upon. I remember feeling especially guilty since I was truly the responsible party and hadn't lived up to the trust that I had been given. A little bit of the carefree quality of childhood was lost that day.

Years later, I recognized the extraordinary guidance my parents and their generation meted out. They instinctively knew when we children had learned, punished and disciplined ourselves and they also knew when to add an appropriate amount of extra discipline. This was an impressive grasp of the psychology of human behavior gained from ancestors and at the school of human experience.

Going Camping

We were four excited friends all around 10-12 years old. Names have been omitted for reasons that will soon become obvious. Anyone who happened to be there and is still alive reading this has my apology up front. We were going camping with my parents in the Mogollon Wilderness. Bumping along for hours in the back of the "Jimmy" over rocky rutted mountain roads, we were dusty and ready for a pit stop. The urgency was building with every jostle and bump.

Mom and Dad were up front in their new, dark green, GMC pick-up with a 'granny low-gear'. Dad had installed hoop staves over the bed and tied a large tarpaulin over these. Next he made a raised plywood platform above the truck bed making room for all our gear underneath. The camping mattresses provided a cushioned place for boys to ride. It looked like an updated covered wagon ready for a pioneering adventure.

In the din of travel across the mountains, we tried to yell for a pit stop. Then we banged on the side of the truck bed, and waved our hands out from under the canvas, but since we couldn't reach the cab, it was all to no avail. We were unable to communicate our urgent situation to my parents in the cab. The noise and rough bumps continued to drown out our repeated attempts.

All of us were so desperate to relieve nature's urges, that we were forced to help ourselves somehow find relief there in the moving truck bed. One-by-one, we crawled out the back of the truck to cling to the tailgate and bumper while taking care of business. Two of us would take turns holding the one hanging out the back for safety and one would pry up a front corner of the tarp to look out and warn of any oncoming traffic. It seemed like a good plan to solve our urgent situation.

As my last friend took his turn, he turned around and announced, as he pulled his pants down further, he also had to do number two. We stoically held him tightly so he could hang his derriere farther out over the bumper. Suddenly, our lookout began to frantically motion to those us in the rear to pull him in. As we complied, he said: "I'm not finished"...and then we all saw the buildings of a mountain town we were driving through as we frantically jerked him and his bare derriere unceremoniously back into the truck bed.

Desperate times require desperate measures. Those of us in the truck bed that day have borne this profound experience in relative silence for many years. It is cathartic to bring it out from under the hoop staves and finally share it.

Desert Fishing

In the late 40s and early 50s, when my family lived together with my aunts' and uncles' families. Everyone pooled their labor and resources to help each family begin farming on acreages both homesteaded and purchased. One aunt and uncle settled on the South side of the highway and another on the North side. At various moments, houses and spaces were shared in pioneering fashion until each family had a good start with its own land, house, utility structures and equipment. It was an ideal world for children, a great admix of siblings, cousins, friends and plenty of places to explore.

All farms in this part of the desert are irrigated with water pumped from deep wells. The water from each well would irrigate a certain number of acres depending on steady output. Most of the pumps were powered by large electric motors, but some Diesel power was also used. It was customary in those days to store the pumped water in artificial ponds called "tanks". These were bulldozed into being by pushing dirt from the inside depression toward the outside edge in a rectangular pattern. The finished tank covered an area ranging from about one half acre up to two acres or more. One large farm nearby had a giant 5 acre tank. The straight sides of the tank rectangle were around 6 to 10 feet tall and could be more than 20 feet wide at the base.

Not only did the tanks store water for irrigation, they were used for recreation and raising fish. The state helped farmers stock them with bass, bluegill and catfish. In fact, these tanks supported a local ecosystem, that otherwise wouldn't exist in the desert. They certainly were well used by the local children.

We had our favorite tanks on each farm. Each tank had features that made it special, like depth for diving, sandy bottoms, clear water, etc. My uncle Orin's farm on the North side of the highway had a favorite tank. It was a large tank with clear deep water, sandy bottoms on one end, and plenty of fish.

There were many wonderful hours shared in and around that tank. We dove, swam, made rafts and had "sea battles". These required long bamboo poles to pry up wads of water plants and mud ammunition with which to bombard the opponent's raft. A battle was won when one raft was cleared of combatants. No matter how muddy and mucky we became, a good dive and swim in the clear cool water would clean us up. Time at the tank usually meant going home respectably clean.

We also would go fishing in the tanks. Once in a while we actually did catch a few fish and that was great fun. When we caught one large enough, it usually became part of a lunch or a supper. One summer day we decide to try our luck fishing. We gathered our poles, tackle, bait, snacks and drinks, put all this in a wagon and made the one mile trek to the tank down the dusty farm roads.

On that particular day, for some reason, the fish were not biting. We tried every rig, hook and bait we had available. They just were not biting anything, nothing worked still or moving, high or low. We boys were just about ready to give up and go home, when someone asked, "Do you think if we tied a burlap sack over the outlet pipe like a net and opened the valve... will any fish come out in it?"

The rest of us instantly knew this was a genius level idea. The fish weren't biting, but they were still in the water, you could see some now and then. Surely they could be netted like that. We went right to work. Fortunately there were always spare burlap sacks of many sizes on a farm. We rounded up several to try for overall fit to the task at hand.

The outlet valve pipe jutted outward from the base of the tank out over a ditch that was used to transport water into the fields. It was about 12" in diameter and made of rusty steel. We slid a large sack over it and fastened it with tight winds of rope around-and-around. Then it was time to try it out. With great effort, we turned the wheel that opened the valve. Water came gushing out and the pressure blasted the sack right off the end of the pipe!

We then held a towheaded boy's engineering huddle and made an impromptu redesign of our sack fastening technology. Two improvements were made beyond the previous rope wrapping. We gathered the extra burlap into ears of cloth, wrapped these and tied them to the valve. Then three of us held the sack while the fourth slowly opened the valve again.

We held our breath, expecting it to fly off again. This time however, it held without slipping as long as the valve wasn't opened all the way. So we let the water run for a while, then closed the valve, and felt the sack. Success! Sure enough, there were a few fish inside, and respectably sized as well! It was a lot of work to tie and untie the sack, but we were so excited our method was working that we became greedy and kept on netting fish.

Focused on the action, we kept hauling in fish for quite a while. Suddenly my uncle's pickup screeched to a stop in front of us, emerging from the cloud of dust, he jumped out and yelled at us, **"What the Hell are you boys doing? Shut that valve now!"**

We returned as prisoners often do, in the back of a truck. Our crime was breaking the cardinal law of the desert. Do not waste precious water. We, like most lawbreakers, left a clue. Ours was the overlooked river of water roaring down the ditch past my uncle a mile away. Our punishment was banishment from the tank for the remainder of the summer, and from each a solemn promise to never open the valve again without permission.

I could tell, though, Uncle Orin was secretly impressed by our hydraulic engineering and resourceful fishing. After he cooled down from discovering the river of wasted water, he said that it was a shame to waste good fish, and that evening the whole family shared a fine fish dinner.

Dad, Stan and Cletrac

Making A Farm

In addition to the three of our related families that began farming in Luna County New Mexico as related earlier, two more of our families chose to settle near Animas in Hidalgo County about eighty miles further Southwest. Uncle Louis, Aunt Lilly and Cousin Clarence left their place near El Paso and bought a farm in the Animas area. They were joined by newlyweds Uncle Stanford and Aunt Ruth who obtained a farm near them.

It was an exciting time to be a kid and to witness all this industrious activity. It was a lot like a continuance of the great Western migration we studied in school, only we were able to participate in it!

WWII veterans could be granted a homestead of one hundred sixty acres, so Stanford, Orin and many of our farming neighbors obtained land to begin farming that way. Some of these homesteaders were able to add additional land to make larger farms. I remember a few that eventually added enough acreage to have a one square mile farm of 640 acres or more.

Starting with uncleared desert land, however, could be a lot of work. The land was usually wild, formidable desert. Transforming that kind of land into a farm took a massive effort. Just clearing one mesquite with its deep roots and hills that formed around it required moving many tons of earth. Bulldozing the mesquite from an area of 160 acres takes a while. Once the brush, rocks and debris was cleared, stacked and removed, the tasks of deep subsoil plowing and leveling began.

All in all, it took months of work in all kinds of weather. It also took a bulldozer, tractors and other equipment. Farming required water, lots of water, so any good farmland had to have access to water and water rights. Water rights are a license to drill, pump and use water on specified acres of land. Without the water rights, no farming could be done in the desert. Drilling deep wells on land with available water rights was absolutely necessary.

Uncle Stanford and Aunt Ruth started out doing this kind of work on land in Animas. They cleared and prepared a farm there. They shared equipment, work and experiences with Uncle Louis, Aunt Lilly and Cousin Clarence. After farming there for a year, Stanford and Ruth decided that land was not good enough. It was too hard, didn't have the nutrients and didn't absorb water properly. The crops they planted grew poorly. Some kind of change was needed. Besides, Ruth and Stan had their first child during that year of farming in Animas. We all drove the approximately 100 miles to see him. My new cousin John was welcomed into the world.

Around 1950, they found some better land in Southern Luna county about 15 miles North of Columbus on the Mexican Border. Shortly thereafter, they started the big move.

It was decided, that Dad and Mom, would move there also and join them in the task of getting the new farm started. The old army Barrack house they had in Animas, originally from the

Deming Army Base, was moved to the new land and placed on a new foundation. Moving took place on the backroads that followed the international border. It was slow going, but a shorter route than taking the highways around. Also it was easier to drive the slow moving farm equipment and heavy loads on that route. In the beginning, our two families were sharing spaces in the plain, frame barrack home. The initial four adults and three children soon became four adults and four children when Cousin David arrived during that first year at the new farm.

Starting to farm in the desert is dirty, dusty work. Once the land is cleared, there is nothing to break the winds that always come, and when they do, the dust flies. I will always remember the feeling of dirt in the eyes and nose and grit in the teeth; all from just being outside in the wind.

As Dad would say, "Without the dirt, there would be no farm." I agreed, and took it all in stride. I shadowed Dad and Stanford when they were doing all of it. It was great to ride on the old war surplus bulldozer Stanford named "Cletrack" in honor of the tracks and the clicking sound they made. I remember the way they started its Diesel engine on cold mornings by pouring ether into the air intake before cranking it. It was all pretty exciting. Once in a while, when they had a chance they would allow me to drive it. I loved the way the big machine turned on a dime when one track was braked. I also loved to push and pull the hydraulic lever to raise and lower the dozer blade or the subsoiler rig.

Dad was a top notch mechanic. He was certified on just about everything, heavy equipment, aircraft and automobiles. I remember touring his old workplaces, Border Equipment in El Paso and United Airlines in San Francisco. Dad had risen to become a supervisor for Aircraft Maintenance. It was Dad that kept all the farm equipment going, until everyone else learned enough to keep it up.

Living together as we all did in close quarters, I learned

something about the heart and human endurance it takes to be a pioneer in that way. One night, I woke up to tiptoe to the bathroom and saw my Uncle Stanford huddled in a corner of the living area on the floor with a blanket wrapped around his shoulders. He was staring into the dark room through the filtered moonlight shaking violently all over. I was terrified to see him like that.

The next day, I mentioned this to Mom and Aunt Ruth. They told me that Stanford had attacks of Malaria that he got in the Philippine Jungles during the war. From that day on I could tell how much it took for Stanford to resume his life after the Bataan Death March and four years in Japanese Prison Camps.

Changes were made every day. Fields were cleared and leveled, wells were drilled, a garage workshop built, trees planted, a tank and ditches constructed, and more. It went on constantly. In a couple of years, it looked as if the farm had always been there.

There came a day after corrals and a stable were ready, when Ruth decided to bring her horse Polly to the new home. Polly had been staying in Anapra with my grandparents during all the moving and farming. Ruth decided to ride Polly across the desert the approximately 75 direct miles rather than transport her in a horse trailer more than 120 miles.

It was exiting to think of Ruth and Polly somewhere out there in the badlands during this long day of waiting. Now the sun was going down and Ruth and Polly had not appeared. I could tell, Stanford, Mom and Dad were growing concerned. Then, when the twilight was changing into night, barley visible on the horizon, the dark silhouette of horse and rider appeared.

I was jumping up and down with joy. Ruth and Polly made it. I knew the farm was real and it was permanent, because it was now good enough to be a new home for Ruth's beloved Polly.

The Tank Where We Sailed

Sailboat Races in the Desert

Around 1950 Mom and Dad farmed with Uncle Stan and Aunt Ruth in Southern Luna County New Mexico near Columbus. I was counting the days until I started the 7th grade at Sunshine School, but there was still half the summer remaining. One of my chores was to feed a flock of geese that lived around the irrigation tank near the house. As I was spreading goose feed on top of the tank banks, a breeze stirred the water, and I imagined holding the tiller of a sailboat as it was sailing across to the opposite bank. Although it was technically a pond, not even a bonafide lake, I easily imagined it as a sea positioned there in the midst of the desert vista.

Later, leafing through my stacks of old magazines, I saw something that could crystallize my imaginings into reality. It was drawing of a sailboat made from two crossed boards threaded through an inner tube and rigged with a mast, boom and sail fastened to the front of the longer board. The boat was also fitted with a rudder and tiller. It was perfect and also a perfect coincidence! Soon I was looking for suitable boards in the wood scrap pile, patching up an old inner tube for flotation and trimming an old piece of canvas into a sail. Later that day, I was able to launch my new yacht. It was an instant success. I was able to master the noble art of sailing well enough to navigate my sailing craft to various points across the tank. It was exhilarating. After a few days of practice, I was beginning to feel like an old salt. I couldn't wait to share my nautical discoveries with friends and family.

One thing about remote living is that it teaches patience. Farm kids had to wait for the next opportunity to get together with friends and cousins. The best tactic was to plead for a drop off or pick-up connected with a periodic supply run to the farmer's co-op or similar event. Every farm kid becomes very skilled at this. The best result was when an extended stay-over could be arranged. That was a major coup. Thankfully, many farm parents are inclined to be somewhat sympathetic to the obvious need for their children to interact with others in society. Therefore, in time, I was able to share my maritime adventures and lure others to my place on a fairly regular basis.

At first, to share sailing with my cousins and friends we tried taking turns, and even doubling up on the inner tube. It was all great fun, but one thought kept recurring. "Wouldn't it be great if we each had a boat?" someone would invariably ask. Shortly after that I set about to duplicate materials for a second boat and that did the trick. It was almost an act of nature as we took the next evolutionary step into sailboat races.

The boats were almost identical, and race outcomes were often due to little nuances of difference. We learned to adjust the air volume in the inner tubes to maximize performance, to tack and jibe with changing wind directions, to lean and balance the boat in a stiff breeze, and match the boom and rudder angles for maximum speed. It became one of the best activities ever.

That memorable summer, a small group of children learned the essence of sailing in the middle of the Chihuahuan Desert, over four thousand feet above sea level. The homemade, self-built boats made from wood scraps and inner tubes, rope and bits of canvas, were inspired by a single drawing in a magazine. Those humble craft, served to create many hours of great fun, and teach skills that have lasted a lifetime for the participants. The flock of geese that shared the water, also learned to stay out of the way!

Bill's Secret Fort

    My friend Bill and his brothers lived on a large farm that was very near an ancient Mimbres ruin located along a now dry river bed. Bill and his brothers were required to work on their farm with the other farmhands, far more than we were, so it was sometimes difficult to spend time with them. On those rare occasions, however, it was always fun to see what ancient artifacts they had found on or near their farm and otherwise what they had been doing in the interim. This time, it was fantastic! Underneath one of their farm tool and equipment sheds, the brothers had been digging tunnels, which they used as their "secret fort". It was quite a construction. They managed to dig two tunnels, each about 10 feet long. These were big enough to stand up in and intersected so one tunnel served as an entrance and had a ladder from above in one end. The other tunnel was the sanctuary, which intersected the first at a right angle. The boys did their best to make it all safe by using wooden beams and posts to support the tunnels here and there.

    Even at my young age I knew they needed enough support to keep the tunnel from caving in. However, I had no idea how much support was enough. The brothers finished the interior with a wood scrap planking floor, hanging blanket partitions and a few furnishings. I stopped and examined the wooden stools they made for seating. Altogether it was an amazing hideaway to have been constructed by boys between 10 and 13 years old. I was certainly impressed. Bill and his brothers were always creative and resourceful.

    That was a great afternoon that I spent with them, much of the time in the hideaway. The brothers also showed me around the rest of their farm out-buildings where they had access to many great resources and tools, which also explained how they could pull off a project this big.

Later we went in their home to see many of the pots, shards, stone implements and beads they had found nearby. At the end of my visit we planned some future meetings both at my home and theirs. Then we spotted the dust on the road. My parents were coming in our truck to pick me up.

Before I could return to visit them in their tunnel fort, though, I heard that one part of it had fallen in and their father made them fill in the rest. My mother reminded me that it was lucky no one was inside the tunnel when it collapsed. I quietly contemplated how it might have happened when I was visiting. Shortly afterward, my family moved thirty miles away to the other side of the county and I didn't see Bill at school anymore. By the time we reconnected in high school, we had both drifted into separate life experiences. Visiting Bill's secret tunnel fort, as it turned out was fated to be the greatest highlight of our acquaintance.

The Farm Bureau Picnic

Each year, the local chapter of the Farm Bureau would sponsor a picnic for all it's members and their families. It was held in the Gila River valley at a place where there was a large grove of Cottonwood trees. This was very exciting to the children, because it was possible to climb and even walk up the tangle of giant tree limbs strewn around the grove by nature. We would run, play and visit with the other children while the adults chatted, and arranged the picnic buffet. Sometimes, there would be semi-organized games like sack hopping, three-legged races, etc. The picnic featured pit barbecue of mesquite smoked beef and pork.

A few days before the event, the barbecue pits were dug and filled with local mesquite wood. When this burned into embers, the meat was lowered into the pits, which were then covered with sheets of metal roofing and left to cook slowly. The smell of the mesquite smoke and barbecue filled the whole grove along the river, whetting everyone's appetite.

The day of the picnic families arrived bringing side dishes and placed them on several large picnic tables buffet style. Coolers full of cold drinks and water were located nearby. Then when everything was ready, the barbecue was raised from the pits by some of the men, using cables which had been strategically placed earlier. By this time all the attendees had worked up quite an appetite.

We lined up in front of the feast to load our plates from the piles of barbecue, and dishes laden with potato salads, pinto beans, green beans, tortillas, chili, enchiladas, tamales, coleslaw, salads, and more. After stuffing ourselves to bursting, we headed for the many tantalizing deserts.

Soon, everyone was sitting on a chair or log, or lying on blankets in the breeze trying to work up energy to move. The children recovered long before the adults and were soon wading through the gravelly stream-bed, and running up and down the tree limbs again.

It was an idyllic day, there was nothing expected of anyone except to share a good time and great food. Everyone had their entire focus on these goals alone in the beautiful natural setting where there were no other distractions. The golden late afternoon sunlight was beaming through the cottonwoods as everyone was packing up to leave, full and content. As a boy, it was always one of my favorite days of the year, ranking up there with Thanksgiving and Christmas.

The Mine

It was a hot summer morning in the desert as my cousin Jerry and I peddled our old bicycles up the rough gravel road of the foothills toward the small mountains. Our goal was to explore an abandoned WWII mine. As the road became steeper and rougher, we finally could only push the bikes and lift them over obstacles. At last we rounded another bend and could see the remains of shacks, tracks and ore cars strewn between the rocks. We dropped our bikes and excitedly scrambled toward these temptations.

After trying to move rusted ore cars down equally rusty track, stabbing piles of ore with old picks and poking into spider and snake infested wooden shacks, we began to inspect the old mine shafts burrowed deep into the mountain. One, in particular, went straight down into the mountain like a giant well. There was an old, dry, rickety looking, wooden ladder still clinging to one side. We tossed rocks into the gaping hole as sunlight angled down and lit their fall for 50 feet or so. Judging by the time it took the rocks to freefall and bounce downward, we guessed the shaft might be 1000 feet deep.

I was shocked when Jerry announced, "I am going down." "No! That would be too dangerous," I protested! "I am going down anyway," he said as he stepped onto the old ladder. I watched in horror, as he descended, the ladder creaked, squeaked and swayed with each step. Thoughts of Jerry's demise raced through my mind as I watched his figure disappear into the gloom of the shaft. Then, there was only the creaks and squeaks of his on again, off again descent. My frequent inquiries about his progress were met with silence from Jerry, but the sounds of his descent continued.

After what seemed to be a long time, I strained to listen for faint sounds below. Then, suddenly I heard crashing sounds coming out of the mineshaft, timber falling, and loud scraping sounds. The crashing finally stopped and a cloud of dust rose out of the shaft drifting into the bright blue sky.

I was frantic. "Jerry!" I yelled over and over, "Are you okay?" "Can you hear me?" Thoughts were racing through my mind. I didn't want to leave too early, although I wasn't sure what I could do. There was no way to attempt a rescue alone. If he was injured at the bottom of the mine, I knew I should race down the mountain for help. I kept yelling and staring through the wisps of dust rising from the shaft. My yells were only met with silence, so I was certain that I should go for help. Still, I hesitated and stayed to keep the vigil a little longer.

Then, as my hope was fading, I saw a slight movement emerge from the gloomy shadows below. Jerry's dust covered head eased slowly into the light as he slowly and carefully made his way upward. I joyfully watched and finally was able to lend a hand to help him off the last rung up onto the ground.

As Jerry set his feet on solid rock all he said was, "That Goddam rickety ladder, broke off before I could get all the way down!" As we made our way home we knew that it would not be wise to share all the details of this adventure with our parents, at least not for a long, long, time.

Riding Calves

Now and then when farm kids get together, they decide to do things without thinking them through. One day, my cousins, a couple of friends, and I were walking by the barn on the farm belonging to Aunt Kate and Uncle Bob. Looking into the corral at the half grown calves, someone in the group said, "Lets ride the calves!"

Soon we were in the corral climbing up to mount the calves and then hanging on to the broad necks and backs as best we could while the calves tried their best to dislodge us. The idea, was to ride as long as possible, then to slide off the back of the gyrating calf gracefully landing on one's feet. Of course, it was also a good idea, to dismount before the calf got any ideas about scraping you against a fence.

Farm calves, on average are calm and docile by comparison to a wild horse. They can though, with enough excitement, become wild enough to make any kid feel like a rodeo rider. After we rode a few, the herd was becoming a little spooked and the calves were harder to approach and mount.

Not to be deterred, I pulled myself up onto the back of one calf and off we went. The calf was gyrating well enough to make it hard to hang on and suddenly I found myself slipping over the rump and off the back end while it was moving fast. I lost my balance landed ingloriously on my rear with a bone jarring thud right in the middle of a large patch of Goat Head vines. I could feel every thorn as it parted from the vine and stuck into my hands, legs and rear end.

Needless to say, my enthusiasm for calf riding ended as suddenly as it began. I began pulling the goat head thorns one-by-one out of my sore hands and backside, while all the other children were laughing uproariously at the sight.

A Memory of Christmas Magic

Early Christmas morning, our family tradition was to drive to the upper Rio Grande Valley near El Paso to celebrate with my dad's parents. Along the way we visited as many of our relatives as possible. We would stop and exchange gifts, visit for a while and then head to the next stop. While the adults chatted and sipped coffee or tea, my sister and I would visit with our cousins. Then, when it was time leave, we would beg to have our cousins join the entourage. Often, since it was Christmas, permission was granted. So onward we went in a full vehicle toward our last stop near the Rio Grande.

That was the Christmas crescendo. All of our near and far flung family members would rendezvous there to celebrate and partake of the huge buffet Grandmother Bond would place on the long dining room table. I imagined it to be similar to a feast in the great hall of a medieval king.

Often several carloads of family arrived simultaneously, with children jumping out of the cars and rushing to greet and be greeted by all. After greeting our grandparents and family members, Grandma would make sure that we each had a glass of eggnog with a proper dusting of nutmeg to sip. Then we dashed off to find cousins not seen recently. The older grandchildren, like myself, would take our eggnog and wander about the house away from the smaller noisier children and the adults gathered in the living and dining rooms.

As we wandered toward the back of the house, the true magic of Christmas happened. Our Grandpa would appear near the back pantry, winking at us from a corner looking exactly like the "Jolly Old Elf" himself, only in khakis rather than red and white. His rotund figure, his rosy cheeks, and his jolly chuckle, added to the picture. He would hold up a finger near his mouth indicating silence, then motion us to follow him into the pantry.

There, he would take a bottle of Jim Beam from a high

shelf, open it and carefully splash just a bit in each of our eggnog glasses. Although it was just symbolic, it was powerful magic. It was his way to confirm our growing up. Indeed, it was a recognition that was more special than any present under the tree.

Afterwards he would whisper, "Merry Christmas," and we would smile a "Thank you," as we wandered off to savor our magic Christmas eggnog and share the wonderful dinner.

Guns and Feet

I had a friend my age who was close to the same size and shared one given name in common with me. "Look", they said at school, "There are the twins." At that time, we were also about the same height, but my friend wore glasses and I didn't.

It was five miles or so to the farm where he lived so we didn't visit very often, but we did see each other at school. Although we always wanted to share more time together for outdoor adventures, chores, homework and other obligations always seemed to get in the way.

Once in a while though, when one of us had some free time, we would walk to the other farm just to see if there was a possibility of sharing some hours hunting or looking for Indian artifacts. It always felt great, if we showed up unannounced and the other was granted permission to do something with their friend for a few hours. Sometimes dropping in like that could yield more than expected. I remember walking the 5 miles across the desert to Scotty's family farm and getting there right when his father was bailing hay. I wound up on the trailer with him stacking scores of hay bails and bringing them to the barn. Only when the bailing was done could we go off on free time.

There was one day we spent hunting rabbits that will never be forgotten. He and I had .22 caliber rifles and were roaming the desert surrounding his family's farm mostly just talking. Stopping to rest, I noticed he had a habit of resting his gun muzzle on the top of his boot. This made me very uneasy, I had been taught gun safety, and that did not include putting a gun muzzle anywhere close to a human body part.

"Scotty," I said, "Do you know that you have the business end of your rifle resting on your foot?"

"I aways do that, to make sure it don't slip into the dirt," he said.

"It makes me nervous," I replied, adding, "You might do it with your finger still on the trigger sometime and the thing might go off on top of your foot."

"Oh no, I've been doing it for a long time with no problem. I won't forget a thing like that," he confidently stated.

"OK." I said as I held my rifle at present arms and resumed walking. In my mind the matter was settled. It was after all, his decision about his own safety.

We kept on then, not so much hunting, but mostly looking for arrowheads in a part of the desert where many had been found over time. I noticed he kept repeating his habit of parking the gun muzzle on that same boot.

Then suddenly, my fears were realized, his gun went off and as he removed the muzzle from the top of his foot, sure enough, there was a small round hole in the leather of his boot surrounded by residue.

Even though, I had stated my fear earlier, it was still a shock to me and he was definitely in shock. He decided to leave the boot on for the journey back home, so he leaned on me and we hobbled back across the mile of desert to his farm. His frantic sister and mom helped him into the car and they took him into town for emergency medical attention.

As I was walking the five miles home, the entire scenario kept replaying in my mind, as well as my father's many lessons on gun safety. I realized, my friend must not have gotten the same lectures, or that he may have not paid as much attention to them.

Later, on crutches, he described the emergency room surgery and the way they tried to remove of all the bits of lead from his foot. Finally, the doctor said that they could not get quite all of it, but they removed as much as they safely could. His foot healed in time, but he always had a limp after that. I thought that was a lesson that would last him a lifetime. However, after I moved away to Arizona, I heard from one of my relatives that he'd actually done it again.

"Some people never learn," I thought. Then the thought continued, "...but many others do learn from the example of someone else." There was never a better example for learning this safety lesson, than my old friend Scotty.

Porky's First and Last Ride

A little albino piglet appeared in a litter one day. It was neglected by the young sow. It had two strikes against it already at birth since it was white in a brown litter, and the runt of the litter as well. The adults said it probably would die soon, but my aunt started feeding it with a baby bottle and soon it attracted the attention of all of us kids. We named him Porky and kept feeding him.

Porky was a smart little rascal. He was soon thriving around the farm house and made himself right at home. A small banket became his starter bed in a safe corner of the house. He hung around with the family and took house training in stride. Letting us know when he needed to go out just took a grunt. As the weather warmed up, he nosed open the screen door and let himself out.

Dad and my uncle Stanford were not so keen on him being a house pet. They kept reminding us that he would soon outgrow that role and become too big to be inside or even be completely trusted. Kids however, don't want to hear of these things. They see the world as it is in that particular moment and at that moment Porky was a twelve-pound piglet.

We would run, play, do chores, and he would be hot on our heels like any other member of the group. Soon he was bossing around all the other animals, the dogs, cats, chickens and geese. They knew not to mess with Porky. All it took from him was a snort or grunt and they gave him due respect. He was a firm, lithe and agile 65 pounds by this time and rapidly gaining.

From time-to-time we were reminded of Porky's inevitable future by one of the adults. Mom and Aunt Ruth were more sympathetic to the bond between kids and animals, but even they had to admit the men had a point. Anyway, for the time being Porky had assumed he was also a kid as he followed us around.

This went on for a time until Porky was getting quite large. We were guessing that maybe he had grown to 200 lbs or so. Indeed, he looked formidable to strangers driving up for the first time. We knew however, he was as docile as a lamb. So life with Porky seemed like it was going on happily into the future, in spite of the dire predictions.

Then one day, everything changed in an instant. No one could have foreseen the way it was fated to happen. It was our big shopping day of the season. The periodic day everyone would get to go to the Farmer's Cooperative in town for groceries and supplies. Dad drove the sedan to the front of the house and as Mom and Dad were climbing into the front, and I opened a back door on one side to enter the car, Porky decide he was going too. He pushed passed me and jumped into the car. There was no room for us kids. Porky took up the entire rear seat area. In fact, he was standing on the floor wedged between the front and rear seats, kind of hanging over the rear seats.

Dad turned around when the car shook from Porky's entry. I could see his face redden as his blood pressure rose. "Get that pig out of the car right now!" He said angrily.

I tugged and pulled on Porky, as I tried to talk him out of the car also. But nothing worked. He couldn't or wouldn't move. Then Dad got out and did the same, muttering under his breath. By that time, Mom had gotten out so no one was in the car except Porky.

Finally Dad said "Everyone get away from the car, and he started shutting the doors, back and front, all except for the drivers door. Then he got in and said, "I will be back soon," as he and Porky drove off in a cloud of dust toward town.

It was one of those shocking, sobering days in life when ideals and reality collide head on. Dad returned without Porky and we went to town in stony silence. All Dad said as we drove away was: "I tried to tell you, but nobody ever wants to listen."

The author riding bareback

Reading in the Saddle

I never felt like a true horseman, but sometimes, I felt like keeping up at least a small connection with the horses that were always around me growing up. When I was 12, I decided to saddle up a gentle mare from the corral and ride her to the mailbox to pick up the mail.

I was proud of myself, I did it all, bit, bridle, blanket, saddle and cinch. No problem, after all I had learned from the best horsewoman in the West, my aunt Ruth. She had me in the saddle since I was a toddler. Now was the time to show myself that I was fully capable of horsemanship any time. The mare and I were soon headed toward the mailbox a short mile away.

After retrieving the mail and the newspaper from last Sunday, I turned the mare around to head back. As she plodded along, it seemed so relaxing that I started to read the folded newspaper. Soon, I found myself tempted to pull out the section of Sunday comics to read. With the reins dropped over the saddle horn, and the mare plodding along, I held the comic section open and read to the gentle swaying of the walking horse.

Suddenly, a strong gusty breeze hit the open paper, rattling it and nearly taking it out of my hands. My docile mare was startled. She was so spooked by the rattling paper that I was flying over her head before I could let the paper go and grab the reins or anything else.

I will always feel that jolt of hitting the ground in a sitting position still holding the comic section. It was spine compressing from tailbone to the top of my head. The mare trotted off leaving me to pick up the remains of the mail blowing around the desert floor. I also picked up my sore frame and the shattered illusions of a life of masterful horsemanship.

I caught up with the mare standing near the farmyard, where she decided to stop after running away. When I lead her back into the corral and removed the saddle and bridle, I was kind of embarrassed with my performance in the saddle. Perhaps, that was the day I started to imagine the kind of life that eventually took me completely away from ranching and farming.

Boys from the Ranch

A few miles from where we lived, up the rising Southwest slope of the Florida Mountains was a ranch house. It was the next stop for the school bus after picking me up. Two brothers around my age, 11 years old got on there. I'll just call them the R boys for the sake of anonymity. The R boys were friendly, ordinary boys in every way. In fact they were quite down-to-earth likable guys, except they had one huge social problem. Their mother made them suck garlic cloves all day.

Simply put, the R boys had a breath that could knock over a charging bull. When they got on the school bus the conversation stopped and everyone looked the other way as to not make eye contact. All the other children tried to double up in the seats ahead of time to make sure they had to keep moving by in search of a place to sit.

The problem was, it wasn't always possible to do that. There was always an age, grade level and personality reason for school kids to pair up, so even a socially normal kid could still be alone in a seat when the bus stopped at the R boys ranch. Also, the rule was you could only move when the bus was stopped. Depending on prior circumstances, any given morning that I stepped onto the bus, there might be an acceptable open seat or there might not.

Therefore, when the fateful stop was made, and the R boys got on there was always a chance I would be alone on a seat leaving room available for one of them. This made for one nerve-wracking experience as the R boys made their entrance down the school bus aisle. I froze in place as the promenade transpired. It seemed like every other day one of them would sit on the outside of the bench seat next to me.

"Hi." the R boy would say as they sat down. "Hi." I would reply as I tried not to breathe or grimace. Then I would quickly turn toward the window to grab a quick breath of air before looking his way again.

Then, he might say, " are you gonna shoot marbles again at recess or lunch?"

I would reply: " Yes, Scott and I are planning to have a shoot out match, wanna play the winner? Oh, Wow!"

R Boy: "Wow what?"

Me: "Wow, your breath is sure strong!"

R Boy: "That's the garlic my mom makes me suck on so I won't catch anything."

Me, grimacing: "That breath will kill a bull, you won't catch anything at all." Then I would turn toward the window again to catch my breath, while hoping for a bit of uncontaminated air before looking back toward him again.

Not only would the smell get me but, my eyes would water like I was around peeled onions. It was going to be a long ride. Almost an hour from their ranch to the school on the route the bus took. During one such encounter, a few days earlier, the R Boy showed me the pocket full of garlic cloves his mom supplied them with for the day. When one became too well sucked upon, it was to be discarded and replaced with a new one. This was supposed to go on all day.

I felt kind of sorry for them, since I knew I wasn't the only kid who had trouble with their odiferous breath. But even so, I couldn't bring myself to volunteer to sit with them. Not only that, there was a possibility that I might have to sit by one on the way home too. I always wondered, if the R boys were to stop sucking garlic, "Would their breath odor ever clear up again?"

The Cutting Horse

My friend Scotty had a rare day off and invited me over to spend the time together just having fun. At some point during the morning, he asked me to go horseback riding with him. I said, "OK," and we saddled up two suitable steeds. Our ride started out uneventfully as the horses trotted along, mine alongside his. It was a very nice day for a ride. The sun was shining and there was a gentle breeze to counter any rising temperature. Our horses were well rested and ready to go. It was open range, so there wasn't much except creosote and sagebrush to hinder us.

We came to a dry lake bed that was very open and flat, so we urged our horses into a gallop. After a time, it seemed like the horses had galloped long enough so I slowly pulled the reins signaling my horse to slow down. Not being very experienced with horses, I also gave a steady list of all the verbal commands, I could think of, beginning with "Whoa!" stated with as much authority as possible. This was followed by more "Whoa! Stop! Stay! Halt!" I noticed that Scotty had already slowed his steed down and started turning his horse around. Meanwhile, my horse was still going at full gallop, and I was beginning to worry about exhausting him. I had visions of the horse dying in mid gallop and collapsing while I flew off into the desert! It was becoming a nerve-wracking, scary thought.

I tugged and tugged on the reins while repeating the verbal commands, but the horse simply ignored my efforts and kept right on at full speed. Finally, I decide to attempt turning him around at a gallop, so I pulled to the left toward the direction I last glimpsed Scott heading. The horse stopped so fast, that I had to hold on for dear life to avoid losing my balance and slipping over his head. What a surprise. I hadn't experienced that kind of thing before. But I was glad that he stopped.

After a short time, the horse and I were finally headed a

good bit slower toward our companions waiting on us about a quarter mile away. As we drew up to them, I said, "I never was on a horse that didn't know how to stop before".

Scotty replied, "I forgot to tell you, he is a cutting horse, the Mexican guy we got him from trained him to stop on a quick left jerk". "Thanks for finally letting me know," was all I could think to say as we continued the cool down journey back to the corral for some much needed water.

The Dutch Oven

In the Fall, the men in my family had the tradition of going deer hunting. They would gather and plan out the event at one family farm a week or so prior to the opening of the season. One of the big decisions was where to hunt. New Mexico is a big state with many federal and state lands to choose a hunting location from. Either my dad, my uncle Orin, or my uncle Stan would start planning the year's hunt, joined by the others, including other uncles, family friends and fellow farmers. As the boys in the families grew to a certain age, they were invited to come along.

Unlike forest hunting, where hunters are in a tree stand along a game trail, the hunting we did involved lots of hiking in rugged terrain. A day's hunt covered miles of distance in high mountain canyons. This meant choosing a proper location where everyone could spread out and comb some mountainous terrain and fire at game without endangering each other. In short, the number in the hunting party had a lot to do with choosing a location.

Then of course, there was all the general logistics of transporting everyone and everything needed for the camp. Who was riding with whom, where everyone would sleep, and what food to bring, and so forth. Planning could take a while and require drinking several beers, until all the details had been figured out.

The day the hunt began, it was required to leave really early, like say 4 AM. It was important to arrive at the destination before sunrise, spend the day hunting and get back to the campsite while there was enough daylight to set up camp. Everyone usually ate sandwiches and various snacks like hard-boiled eggs, jerky and Vienna sausages during the day. The second day of the hunt, began with eggs, bacon, potatoes and toast cooked over a campfire or Coleman stove at dawn. Then the men would put something in a Dutch oven and bury it in the coals to simmer all day while we were hunting. We would bring sandwiches, snacks and a canteen of water to consume on the hunt.

One particular time, the Dutch oven was filled with pinto beans, pork and chili, covered with enough water to simmer and steam all day. We left for the hunt with visions of a good meal of camp pork and beans to devour by the flickering campfire that evening. No bucks were seen or taken all day, but we all remembered the great feast simmering in our Dutch oven.

That day we hunted three long canyons with ridges rising up to about eight thousand feet. There were eight of us, so for the first two canyons we had one person on each ridge and one in the bottom. The remaining canyon was covered by one hunter in the canyon, and one on the ridge that offered the best view.

As the hot Dutch oven was lifted from the coal bed, all of us hungry hunters clutched our metal camp plates in eager anticipation. The lid was lifted treating us to the lovely aroma of hot chili pork stew. Meanwhile, one of my uncles was heating tortillas on a grill to go with the meal. Ladlefuls of the steaming goodness were placed in the awaiting plates and we all found a seat around the warm fire in the crisp, evening air.

Then one, by one the comments started. Someone said, "My beans aren't done!"

Then, the next voice added, "Mine aren't either, they're still kind of hard!"

Followed by, "Mine, too. Does anyone have beans that are cooked enough?"

It was determined that everyone had a plate full of half cooked beans. Some of which had already been ravenously devoured. Then the discussion went to what to do about it. Should we all scrape our plates back into the Dutch oven and cook it all some more or what?

Uncle Orin said. "Look, we have all eaten some already

while we have been discussing the issue, and the beans are chewable, they are just a little dry in the middle, so I think we are safe just finishing them up. If we cook them again, it will be midnight before we get done with supper."

That seemed reasonable enough to the rest of us, so we did just that. We finished our supper, which actually did taste pretty darn good after hunting all day in the mountains. Afterwards we straightened up camp and headed to our sleeping bags for some well-earned rest.

I awoke in the middle of the night with a sharp pain in my left side. For a moment, I lay looking up at the bright moon painting the camp like daylight. Then I felt it again, more intense this time. Suddenly, I was grabbing a wad of paper and running up the hill, without even lacing my boots.

After obtaining relief from the immediate, acute intestinal pain, I stumbled shivering back toward my sleeping bag, when I noticed others were also behaving in a similar fashion. Indeed, the whole campsite was full of moaning, restless people.

I heard a number of stomach noises, accompanied by remarks like, "Damn, we shouldn't have eaten those *%^&$# beans!", and, "Crap, I hope we don't all die before daybreak!" This kind of behavior followed by vomiting and general misery went on the rest of the night. Needless to say, dawn broke upon a sorry lot of sick campers. All the purging, at least, seemed to diminish the general pain and discomfort.

Sunrise came and nobody felt like hunting, or anything else, so the decision was made to pack up and go home. No one could eat a bite of breakfast either. We drove the hours back in miserable silence. "That Dutch oven full of partly cooked meat and beans saved the lives of several deer this season," Dad remarked, as we drove through our driveway gate.

The Little Mountain Range

We finished a big, delicious lunch, enjoyed by everyone. Fresh fried chicken, piles of steamed and buttered corn on the cob, green beans, biscuits and watermelon. All of us were very full, and Cousin Jerry and I were sitting on the front porch feeling very satisfied.

As we looked across the desert to the Northeast, we saw a small range of mountains in the distance. We realized that although we saw them every day, we didn't know what they were called. Nevertheless, they held sufficient mystery to call out to us with their siren song that afternoon.

"Have you ever been to those little mountains?" I asked Jerry.

"No," he replied.

After a brief discussion, we decided they were only ten or fifteen miles away, so why not walk on over to check them out? It seemed to be a sensible enough plan. After all, we were young, curious, full and healthy, so why not?

We grabbed a little water and set off walking at a fast pace. As we ducked between the strands of barbed wire at the edge of the rangeland we looked in the direction of the mountains and headed more or less to the middle of them. We doggedly kept on, crossing flat range, railroad tracks, several arroyos of various sizes, changes in rangeland elevation, changes in flora, more barbed wire fencing, herds of grazing and resting cattle, several jack rabbits and a couple of disturbed rattlesnakes.

After a few hours, and well into the afternoon, we were getting visibly nearer to the mountain range. Details were becoming more distinct, one could see canyons, ridges, and vegetation here and there. These were important features if there was time to climb them before turning back. We discussed what particular part of the range looked the most promising and picked up the pace toward that area.

It hadn't been very long, when we spotted what looked like a ranch house in the distance. It was located toward the foothills of the range in the general direction we were going. As we grew closer to it we could see it was abandoned. It was a ghost ranch to be sure. We walked up to it and explored the area. It obviously had been abandoned for decades, there were no signs of life or even recent tracks of any kind around or in the house. Doors were open, windows missing, and it was generally in disrepair. Enough small items were strewn around the vicinity to determine it had once been a homestead rather than a ranch. Abandoned most likely for a lack of water and therefore crops to sell. There was a calendar still hanging on one wall inside dated 1929. That sort of told the rest of the story.

After hanging out there in the house for a while, we went back out and looked at our original goal, the mountain range. The slopes began to rise a short distance East of the abandoned homestead. Even though the heat of the day had peaked, and the sun was lower, we decided to claim our bragging rights and pressed on.

Thankfully, the mountains, were not very tall and were somewhat rounded in shape. Just before sundown, we stood triumphantly on the top of one of the higher rises. We took a brief look around, took our bearings, and began a rapid, lopping descent. I think we knew that we couldn't make it all the way home before dark, but we were determined to try.

The further we went, the darker it became. We were waiting for the moon to rise and help us out, but it never came. Of course, it had to be a moonless night on the portion where we needed it most. Soon, we were stumbling and running into brush. It was a little scary thinking of stepping on a rattlesnake unseen in the darkness, but since we were making enough noise to clear out the wildlife, truthfully breaking a leg or spraining an ankle was probably a greater danger.

The highlight of the journey back, was the moment I took a step and my foot came down on thin air. I found myself plunging off the steep side of an arroyo. Thankfully it was only about a five foot drop, but it was exhilarating to be sure. Jerry managed to avoid that one by being a few hundred feet to the left of me at a somewhat less steep embankment.

We kept our sights on the distant lights scattered about the little farm community and kept going. We were very careful to be aware of any barbed wire fence. It could be disastrous to run into one in the dark at full walking speed. Fortunately, we had just enough starlight to make them out on the occasions we approached one.

We didn't know how long we had been walking, stumbling across the desert, but finally, we crossed the last fence and stepped back onto a farmers road. What a relief, it was a mile or less to make it home!

As we walked up to Jerry's home, we saw the lights still on in the house. Entering we saw, four anxious parents, a table full of coffee cups and flashlights. It was the wee small hours of the morning. Our afternoon walk had taken us about fifteen hours.

We were chastened and forgiven. Everyone turned in to get a very little sleep in what was left of the night. It was sure great to be back safely I thought as I pulled up the covers and remembered, "Damn it, I should have taken that calendar off the wall for a souvenir when I had the chance!" Sometimes, one does experience regret.

TJ

Assume for each person on the Earth, there is another person who is an energy opposite. By that I mean, someone who cannot share space or time with you without an explosion occurring. In my life so far, this theory has manifested itself once.

There were three boys in my class, besides myself, from the 5th through the 8th grades. Two were my friends, the third was not. His name was TJ. We were both small, close to the same size, and somehow we would automatically fight, if we got close to each other. This was not explainable, just simply spontaneous combustion.

The teachers had to put us on opposite sides of the room to keep the peace. We each were assigned to opposite sides of the schoolyard at recess. The school personnel kept us successfully separated for three years. At eighth grade graduation, we were placed on opposite sides of the stage. Then we went our separate ways.

The summer after grade school, I forgot completely about TJ. In the fall, I started high school. It could not have been a more complete distraction. I went from a class of nine students, to one of over one hundred. Grade school was always in one room. In high school, every class was in a different room. It was all so new and exciting. TJ never entered my mind at all the entire school year.

Then one day, I visited the boy's room to relieve myself. I was standing at one urinal attending to my business. For some reason, I glanced to my right and discovered that the person at the next urinal was TJ. He saw me at the same time.

We both finished, both zippered up, turned toward each other and without a word being said, started fighting. We pounded, hit, kicked, pushed, shoved and then did it some more. Then suddenly it was over. Men were pulling us apart and telling us to stop fighting. Having overheard the commotion, the shop teacher, and the janitor rushed into the room. Afterward, they took us to the principle's office.

I was put on suspension for a week and then my life slowly became like it was before the encounter. I didn't see TJ any more. He vanished from my life and I from his. Strangely, he never entered my thoughts except the exact moments we encountered each other. I have always been puzzled as to why we behaved like that together.

Thankfully, I never experienced such encounters with any other person in my life. It remains a mystery. There was no seething verbalized hatred. There were no threats, no build up, no planning, or bullying. It was unverbalized yin and yang, like opposite electric forces, which explode in close proximity and on contact.

Soda Shop Malts

    I attended four classes each morning- Algebra, History, English and Civics. Halfway through the morning, in English class, my stomach would growl and I would start looking forward to lunchtime. It became harder and harder to concentrate on studies after that. Lunchtime was the highlight of my high school day.

    It was a great ritual. At the sound of the lunchtime bell, we all bolted to put away books in lockers, grab our lunch bag and then head out the door to the street. Walking fast or jogging, we traversed the ten blocks or so to the city drug soda counter. The goal was to get there before the crowd so you would have plenty of time to relax and enjoy your chosen confection prior to heading back to class. It was a way to exercise, socialize and reward oneself for a morning of work behind a desk.

    All the way down the sidewalks to the soda counter, I dreamed of the tall glass filled with the blended ice cream treat, topped with whipped cream and a cherry. The freedom of lunch period, if timed well, could encompass both lunch at the soda shop and a short visit to the bookstore or hardware store before heading back to afternoon classes.

    There are shake people and there are malt people. I discovered at the soda shop, that I was a malt person. Actually the two confections are identical except for the scoop of malt powder tossed into the malt. Somehow that scoop of toasted barley made the ice cream and milk taste so much better to me. It added an extra dimension of flavor beyond that of mere ice cream. It was so gratifying to see the soda jerk scoop the ice cream, add the liquid and toss in the scoop of malt before blending the mixture. Finally, the icy froth was poured in a tall glass, topped with whipped cream, a cherry and placed in front of you on the counter. My peanut butter sandwich and malt lunch was magnificent. It gave perspective to the day and energy to see me through afternoon classes and the long bus ride home.

Choices

It was another hot summer day in the desert. We walked in between the large rows of cotton plants with sharp hoes looking for the weeds that would compete with the cotton for water and nutrients. Until the cotton grew too high, the rows were cultivated with a tractor that would remove the weeds in the furrows. However, there was no machine available that could remove the weeds intertwined with the plants on top of the rows. That work was done by hand. My family believed in avoiding weed killing chemicals if at all possible. So we walked, chopped and pulled. We sometimes hired workers to do the same.

Dad would say, "If it poisons any plant, it isn't good for any other plant to be exposed to it and it isn't good for the environment either." He would always choose a natural way to control weeds and insects before turning to a chemical. He did not like the way humans interfered with nature.

Mom and I had been chopping all morning and our stomachs were signaling that it was getting close to lunchtime. Usually, she would stop weeding and go to the house to prepare an easy lunch for the rest of the family. This time she posed a question, "Would you like to make some lunch today or should I go do it?"

She must have had an instinct for the situation. I was ready for the suggestion to go into shade and find something cold to drink. "I will do it. What should I make?" I said.

"Fideo or tuna salad sandwiches would be good," She replied, then she added, "...or if you want to start cooking some ground beef for tacos, I can help finish them when I get in."

"OK, I am on my way," I stated as I shouldered the hoe and headed to the house.

I leaned the hoe on the porch, went in the kitchen door, hung my hat on a hook, grabbed a glass from the rack and filled it with cold well water at the sink. I gulped down a couple of glasses of the cool water, and then got to work. I decided to start making fideo, which I loved. The combination of toasted vermicelli, galric, chili, tomatoes and cheese were delicious.

Seeking the ingredients I walked back and forth from the cabinet to the counter a few times, and stopped at the sink for another glass of water. As I set the water glass down again, I discovered, I was not alone in the kitchen. A tail was sticking out from under the sink cabinet just enough to see a full set of rattles on it!

I eased slowly back, stepping carefully, adrenaline pumping. "Holy Cow! I thought, "It is really good I didn't step on it before I saw it!"

I shuddered as I thought about the casual walking around I did when I didn't know it was there. I could have stepped on it any number of times.

"Why didn't it rattle?" I thought, "Is it dead? Is it asleep? How can I get it out? I'm not going to reach down and pull it out by the tail!"

Instinctively, I went into the hall and grabbed a broom. Then I stuck it as far under the cabinet as I could a short distance away from where I could still see the tail. Then I gave it a quick low sweep. Out came a medium size, angry, rattlesnake into the middle of the kitchen vinyl floor. It was striking at the broom and then it uncoiled and tried to slither back toward the cabinet.

Quickly, I swept it toward the hall and the back door. I had to firm up my grip each time the broom pushed the snakes weight a little further. It was a great relief to see that it was only the screen door I had to maneuver the snake through. That still could be a challenge.

Finally, the angry snake was coiled against the screen door. I took the broom handle and cautiously reached over the snake to push the door open a bit. The snake took the opportunity to slither out onto the porch.

Watching through the screen door, I waited until it

located itself away from the doorway, and then I went out to grab my weeding hoe. It was not desirable to have a rattlesnake hanging out right around the house, so I scraped it off the porch and dispatched it with my hoe.

    Mom and Dad missed the action, but I left the evidence to support my confession as to why lunch was late. Even though our meal became somewhat delayed, it was peacefully enjoyed without any more uninvited guests.

College Pigs

I was working out on the Arizona farm with my dad. We had been row-binding the field corn and stopped to take a water break. Dad gestured toward the 5 acre apple orchard nearby. "This is going to be your college." He said.

What he said was quite a surprise. So far, in my young life, I'd never had one serious thought about college. "What do you mean?" I asked, trying to sound composed.

He said: "We are buying some feeder pigs today to put in the orchard. You are going to raise pigs until you finish high school and then auction them to pay for your college studies. The corn we are harvesting now is what you will feed them with this season."

"Where should I go to college?" I asked. Dad simply replied, "You will figure it out by then. Lets get back to work".

That long ago morning in Arizona was a truly empowering moment. The best confirmation a boy could have. My father, in one second, had empowered me to finish high school and send myself to college at the same time. In that moment, an unfocused child instantly began the transformation into a young man who was definitely going to college and needed the grades and goals to match. Looking back, it is also obvious that the better grades I earned the next two years, resulted from the new direction my life took on that day.

Of course, the work and discipline connected to raising the pigs was also part of my education, although I realized that part much later. The corn we fed the pigs was grown on a field, with water rights, that was not used for growing cotton, or feeding cattle. I would stockpile the sheaves of corn for the season in the pole shelter, where I also fed the pigs and penned the sows and piglets.

I learned about distributing food and clean water, keeping the pens cleaned, boars and other sows separated from the piglets, and many other details connected with raising healthy animals. Sometimes, newborn pigs were abandoned, and required bottle-feeding. It seemed a slower process than it actually was, but the number of pigs grew steadily along with the number of gilts and sows.

After each sale my college fund grew also. When it was time to leave for college, all the pigs were sold. I withdrew one hundred forty dollars from the fund to buy a used 1947 Chevy coupe. In it, my best friend and I journeyed off to begin college in Los Angeles. Raising pigs for two years turned out to be a trade for two years of college.

Insect Collecting

My high school biology teacher assigned the class one of the best projects I had ever encountered. We were to make an insect collection. Careful directions were given regarding the collection, preservation, identification, mounting, storage and presentation of the specimens.

After acquiring the net and collection supplies, I eagerly began to collect specimens. At first, it was relatively easy to find them. However, after the common insects were collected it became increasingly more difficult to find the unusual or somewhat rare specimens.

The Palo Verde Beetle and the Horned Scarab were great finds. As was the Luna Moth, which I was fortunate to find freshly expired. It was the kind of project that motivated students to do well. In fact, there was a competitive spirit among our classmates to see who could find, mount and display the specimens from the greatest number of insect groups.

I would go outside with my collecting bottles and net early each morning before school and again right after coming home each afternoon. Often, I would go out hunting for specimens once more just before dark and finally net insects around the porch light before bedtime.

At sunrise one morning, I took my gear out in front of our house to look around. It was then, I saw the biggest moth I had ever seen sitting still with wings folded sitting on a flowering plant very near the front porch. Its back was toward me as it faced the morning sun.

My heart was pounding as I crept silently toward it slowly raising the net. I knew that no one else would have such a wonderful specimen as this. I could hear the comments from my classmates and the teacher already. "If only I can make this catch," I thought. "Maybe, it is a kind of moth that just came north from Mexico." My imagination was running wild as I continued my stealthy approach.

Then, I made my move, swinging the net as fast and as smoothly as I could. Success! When the net came around, I clearly saw my catch for the first time and it was not happy. In fact, it was trying to attack me through the net!

It was then, my bubble burst. I hadn't caught a rare giant moth, at all. Rather, it was an extremely pissed off hummingbird! It was promptly freed from the net, and I resumed my day with a more realistic view of my collection. I made an 'A' on it anyway.

A Long Lost Grandfather

No one in the family had seen or heard from Grandfather Jundt, my mom's father, for several weeks. My mother and her sisters were at wits end worrying about him and speculating as to where he might be. It wasn't unusual for him to travel or even to be gone for several days at a time. He made his living buying and selling farms, ranches and undeveloped land. He would often travel around in that business. Sometimes he would even stay for a while on this property or that property, puttering around to make some improvements prior to selling it. Our family was used to this being normal behavior. This time however, he hadn't shared his plans or even called to say where he had gone.

Mom and Aunt Pat were on the phone and I heard Mom say, "We could report him missing if we just could decide where or which state he is missing from. He has property all over." Then I heard her say, "When Archie and I get back from Tucson, I will call you again and we can decide, that is if no one has heard anything." Finally, she ended with, "OK, you tell Mom what we are going to decide, so she won't worry." I knew then, Pat would keep Grandmother informed.

The next day, Mom and Dad had to go to Tucson on business, and my little sister was spending the night with her friends, so I was home alone. It was a day of relative peace and quiet with only a few chores to do. As I was in the kitchen, getting a snack out of the refrigerator, the phone rang, so I picked up the receiver and said, "Hello." "Who is this? Is this Arthur?" the voice on the other end inquired.

I immediately recognized the voice. "Grandpa!" I said, "Where are you?"

"I'm in Safford. Can you come and get me?" he said.

"Dad and Mom went to Tucson in the car, but I could

come in the pickup," I replied.

"OK," he said, "Can you come now?"

"As soon as I fill the pickup with gas," I said, but then quickly added, "Where in Safford are you?"

"I'm at the hospital, in the front lobby," he stated. "Are you alright?", I asked.

"Just a few scratches, I had trouble with my truck," he said.

"I'll be there as soon as I can," I reassured him as we hung up.

Safford was a town about forty miles away around the mountain, so I had plenty of time to wonder about Grandpa on the drive up. I arrived at the hospital and found him pacing around the waiting room, with his head bandaged and his right arm in a sling. There was a nurse, trying to get him to sit down and take it easy, but he would have none of it. All he wanted was to get out of there.

When he saw me walk in, his face lit up, and he went over to the side of the waiting area and picked up his old suitcase with his good hand. I rushed over to grab it from him as he was walking out the door. After I put the suitcase in the pickup bed we climbed in and headed back to our farm.

On the way out of Safford, I asked if he wanted anything to eat or drink. "No, lets just get the Hell out of here," he said, "Those doctors and nurses make a big deal out of any little scratch and blow it way out of proportion."

"What did they say happened to you?" I asked.

"A fractured arm and a couple of ribs, I guess. But, I don't think I have any concussion like they said, just maybe a cut and a little bruise on my head," he said. "I'll be fine in a few days with a little rest," he mused.

I inquired, "How did it all happen?"

He said, "My pickup ran off the road and turned over."

"Wow!" I replied, "It's lucky you weren't hurt worse. Did

someone hit you?"

"No, something happened with my truck. It was just a freak accident. Maybe I got light in my eyes and got a little distracted," he said.

As we drove on, I began to piece the story together. Grandpa had been looking at land in Western Canada, and just forgot to call home. That is why the family hadn't heard from him. He got all the way back to Arizona, where he intended to check on his farm in Benson on the way back to New Mexico, before he had the accident.

We made it back to our family farm North of Willcox. When Mom and Dad came home they discovered where he was and had been. Soon the party lines were buzzing between all the family phones. Grandpa had returned in a dramatic way. he stayed with us for a few days until he could get back to New Mexico and fully recover.

Grandpa's wounds healed in time and eventually he was able to travel around again managing his real estate business for a few more years. As far as we knew, he never went as far as Alberta or Saskatchewan again. He also never admitted any fault in regard to the accident near Safford that day, but I knew and so did the rest of the family, that he drove all the way back from Canada to Safford, and then fell asleep at the wheel.

The Speech

One of my classes during my senior year of high school was Public Speaking. I wish I could say it was my favorite class, but like many people, I was gripped with fear at the prospect of getting up in front of a group and speaking. Sure, I heard all the teachers and my parents deliver various reasons for taking a speech class. The standard reason was, "It will give you self-confidence." A lamer assertion was, "It will do you good." The longer reasons usually started with, "In today's world, every professional needs to learn public speaking, blah, blah, blah.." None of these seemed to be convincing to the adolescent mind.

In the end it was my Aeronautics instructor, who taught my favorite subject and also was my favorite teacher, told me I should take it. Thinking back, now I realize, he just wanted to teach speech instead of some other dry subject the Principle was ready to assign him. He just needed the enrollment, and students like me were pushovers to enlist. So I found myself taking Public Speaking in spite of my best instincts and my deep seated fears. Anyway, I was not alone, there were about twenty others taking it also.

Most of the class wasn't too bad, it actually was interesting to study the theory and history of speaking. It was even bearable to stand and read passages from notable speeches. As the semester moved along and the requirements for speaking increased, the fear factor increased as well. The big day came, when the final speech assignment was given. This was the big one that most of us were dreading, the one we wished was over before it even began.

There were a few lucky students who already were comfortable getting up in front of a group and saying just about anything. Most of these were girls, already years ahead of boys in maturity, or boys who had inherited the speech gene, like the sons of local politicians. There were one or two Eagle Scouts who had every merit badge connected with speaking. The rest of us were farm kids like myself, who occasionally spoke to our parents and to livestock. This was scary stuff to us.

The first step was to choose a topic, write a prospectus on it and get it accepted. I thought and thought about what in the world I would have any chance speaking about and sounding like I knew something about it. In short, what could I say to the class that wouldn't sound completely ridiculous?

Finally, the light bulb went off. I was thumbing through old magazines and saw an article on dueling. "That's it!" I thought, "I can at least talk about Alexander Hamilton and Aaron Burr, and maybe I can pad the speech with a couple of old Kings or someone like that." After going to the library and looking up the topic, I wrote my prospectus and got it approved.

"Maybe I will live through this after all," I told Mom.

"I was always confident you would," she said.

"Mom, you always say that," I protested.

The next day I went back to the library and started my research. I couldn't believe how many kinds of duels there had been through history. Dutifully, they were all included in my notes. Soon I had a lengthy and satisfying outline, hopefully, enough to make a speech of the required length. In my teenage mind, this was going to be an important speech. It might be one to go down in history along with the Gettysburg Address. After all, dueling was a serious matter. Lives, countries, and kingdoms were in the balance when duels were arranged.

The speech was written and re-written, read silently, read out loud, read to my parents, read to the wall, recited in parts, recited in longer parts, recited to my parents, delivered to the pigs along with their corn, until it was becoming more and more familiar.

Finally, the big day arrived, the final speeches were to be given in alphabetical order. This meant that my speech was number three. At least, I could get it over with the first day and maybe not get so nervous as those scheduled for the second or third day.

When my name was called, I tried mightily to keep focused and perform all the steps required. First, I walked as slowly and dignified as possible up to the teacher's desk on the side of the room and delivered a copy of my speech, then I turned and walked to the podium, placed my notes upon it, and remembered to look up at the audience, introduce myself, greet them and introduce my topic. God, that was hard to accomplish with fear holding me by the throat! Beyond that, I only remember bits and pieces.

Gripping the sides of the podium with white knuckles, I started my speech, trying to remember not to get in a hurry. After introducing the concept of using dueling as a means for settling differences and matters of honor, I finally started to list examples of dueling from different times and places. My delivery was as serious and solemn as the subject itself. Verbally plodding through my notes, I spoke about duels with guns, swords, knives, and I had come to matters of balance and bodily functions being involved. I was so focused on my notes, and not forgetting anything, that I had forgotten to look up at the audience for a while. It was right in the middle of tickling duels in the Pacific Islands with ostrich feathers, that I remembered to do this.

Pausing, to look up while hoping I hadn't been penalized for the lapse, I found no one out there was looking at me. They had their heads turned in all directions laughing uproariously, pounding on desktops and knees. The teacher, was literally rolling on top of his desk with his head in the middle of the desk pad, hands slapping alongside.

I was so surprised, I just stopped speaking for a time, while everyone came back to their senses. Then I realized, what I had taken so seriously, was comedy for others. My topic had completely redirected the audience from me to it. Suddenly, it was possible to relax. There was no concern about me at all. After the unrehearsed pause I slowly continued on until my speech was completed. Finally, I said, "Thank You," and sat down.

My speech earned an 'A' both for the assignment and for the term. This was not because there were no mistakes, rather it was because my topic prevented them from being noted. I learned quite a lot in Public Speaking Class, and somewhere on the journey I realized public speaking was a little bit less scary now.

College Football

It was the first time I had driven so far from home. I borrowed my parent's car for the evening to attend a football game in Tucson over eighty miles away. It was a cold day in November 1956. This was the first college football game I had ever attended, and I was filled with eager anticipation. First, I drove about thirty miles from my home to pick up my friend Rod, then we headed for Tucson together. The University of Arizona was scheduled to play Arizona State University, a rivalry that provided enough incentive for us to order tickets and make the trip. Rod and I were high school buddies planning to attend college in California, and this outing was a good warm up. We were enjoying our senior year to the maximum.

It was always fun to hang out with Rod, he was more socially advanced than I was. That meant he had an easy time talking to girls. Maybe it was because he came from a large family surrounded by siblings including both older and younger sisters. An added bonus was his appearance. He wore a 'James Dean' ducktail haircut nicely shaped with butch wax. He was constantly looking in the mirror and combing it into shape, knowing that when girls looked at him they were thinking, "James Dean is here!"

By comparison, I was somewhat shy and awkward in social situations. Further, I thought that applying butch wax once a day to my crew cut was quite enough commitment to one's hair and looks. The term for people like myself in those days was 'square'. It was fun to see Rod in action though, and there was a remote chance some of his social graces might be acquired through osmosis.

When we made it to the stadium parking lot, a cold wind was blowing and we knew it would be a chilly evening. At least we had remembered to bring our jackets. We presented our tickets, entered the stadium and then headed toward the open seating section where people were already gathering. I pointed out some empty spaces close to the playing field, but Rod said, "Let's go up there." He pointed to the upper tiers of seating. Then I saw the reason why he was making that suggestion. There were two girls seated up in that area. Soon we were sitting behind them, with Rod already making casual conversation with of the one of the girls.

By the end of pre-game activities, Rod moved down to sit with the girls and I followed. Of course Rod sat next to the more attractive one, and they scooted over leaving space next to the second girl for me. That was the beginning of an awkward evening as fate created pairs of the socially advanced and the socially challenged, respectively. I was so nervous about this situation that honestly the only thing I remember about the game is that the home team lost. That became an omen for the rest of the evening.

Although, we were all wearing coats, I could see that the girl next to me was quite a bit larger than I was and that applied to all three dimensions. I was about five feet nine and 140 pounds for reference. As I glanced at my companion I heard my mother's voice saying, "It doesn't matter how anyone looks, it is their personality that counts." Then, my own inner voice tried to keep being positive, "She is not my type, but maybe she's very nice. I should at least try to talk to her."

That attempt revealed the fact that both of us had the curse of shyness. Our initial attempts to converse made this painfully clear. After exchanging awkward introductions, we sat still with an uncomfortable silence between us. "Thank God, for the noisy football game," I thought.

Finally, I gathered up enough courage, turned toward her and asked, "Which team are you hoping will win?"

"I don't know," she replied, "Who's playing?" This was typical of the bumbling exchange we tried intermittently as time dragged on for us. At least I learned her name was Susan.

Meanwhile, Rod and the other girl, who's name was Linda, were chatting and laughing like old friends. These two very different situations continued until the end of the football game. Rod and Linda were obviously experiencing something far different than my companion and I were. After the game ended and people were making their way out of the stadium, Rod made a suggestion, "Why don't we all go sit in the car to warm up and talk for a little while? Maybe, we can enjoy the rest of the evening."

Somehow I had a sense of dread as the girls agreed and we walked toward my parent's car. Rod and Linda climbed into the back seat and Susan entered the passenger side across from me. I had to admit, though, it was definitely a temperature improvement over the cold wind after we got in the car. To heat it up faster inside I started it and let it run.

While the heater was warming the air, I turned on the radio and tuned it to a favorite local station. It wasn't long before heavy breathing and other sounds were coming from the backseat. I glanced in the rearview mirror and didn't see anyone, so I knew the other two were low on the seat. I reached over to increase the volume on the radio to drown out more of the embarrassing activity behind me. What I hadn't noticed was the effect this was having on my companion in the front. Suddenly, with a large sigh, she swooned and her heavy head landed on my lap.

Adrenaline pumping, I experienced a moment of sheer unadulterated terror. In the grip of panic, I grabbed the keys and bolted out the car into the cold night running across the parking lot and only stopping when I was a safe distance away. As I was trying to compose myself, I looked back toward the car and saw the two girls getting out, followed by Rod, who looked like he was trying to convince them to stay. I didn't move until the girls turned and walked away.

Only then did I head back to the car. I got back in and

Rod entered the passenger side. Neither of us spoke as I started the car and drove off. When we were finally back on the highway headed home, Rod broke the silence. "What happened back there in the car?" he asked.

"I don't know. I guess we just weren't each other's type," I reflected, as we drove on through the night. We never talked about it again.

Rattlesnake Canyon

Having scrambled up near the second highest peak in the Florida Mountain Range, my cousin Jerry and I took a break before beginning our descent. As we drank from our canteens and ate a few snacks, we decided the shortest route down would be through a canyon we called "Rattlesnake Canyon." We were prone to calling any canyon "Rattlesnake Canyon" after one or more rattlesnakes were seen there. This was a narrow canyon strewn with boulders and rocks of all sizes. Further down however, there were areas of gravelly bottoms with a bit of sand here and there.

We picked our way down the steep walls into the canyon, always aware of the reason the canyon bore its name. Inspecting all the details as we slowly descended, we saw no snakes on the first part of the journey. After we reached the passages with sand and gravel on the canyon floor, we relaxed, feeling like all the rattlesnakes were in their holes and crevices on that day. The truth is they are often nocturnal hunters and rest during hot sunny days.

Suddenly, we heard the telltale rattle of warning. We froze in our tracks, while looking around for its source. After looking all around, we finally spotted it- a large rattlesnake, coiled and rattling about ten feet above our heads on a small ledge in the cliff that formed the canyon wall.

As I started to slowly continue down the canyon under the snake, Jerry started hurling rocks toward it. **"Jerry don't, you might knock it...down!"** I yelled just as the rattler fell right between us. All three of us, rattlesnake included, were panicked and we each bolted a different direction from ground zero. As the adrenaline subsided we were able to resume our trek down the canyon as the snake slithered off in search of a more peaceful perch.

The morning I left home from the front porch

Leaving Home

Being accepted by Northrop Aeronautical Institute in the winter of 1956 was a life changing event. It meant I would be leaving home alone the next Spring to live on my own, and I would need transportation for myself and my belongings. The bottom line was that I needed my own automobile.

Until then, I only occasionally drove the family car or truck, but now I had a bonafide reason to obtain my own transportation. It was heady stuff for a young man living on a farm in Arizona to buy a car, pack it up and move to the middle of greater LA and start college.

Since I had a strict budget for college, new cars were completely out of reach. Finding a reasonable, quality used car in a small, rural community was challenging as well. I was almost ready to give up, when I saw an ad for a low mileage 1947 Chevy coupe.

When I went to see it, I discovered that it was owned by

my high school principle. He sold it to me for $140.00 cash, and it became my transportation to a completely new life.

I will never forget the morning I left home. Thunderstorms had drenched the valley during the night and the lingering clouds helped to make a glorious sunrise over the Dos Cabezas Mountains to the East. The air was clean and crisp. The car was packed the night before and was waiting covered with dew in the driveway. I hugged Mom, Dad and my little sister Judy, climbed behind the wheel and drove from the farm North of Willcox to Cochise to pick up my friend Rod, who decided to share this higher education adventure with me. Soon, with Rod's belongings tossed in the back, we were on our way.

One flat tire, one overheated radiator and 600 miles later, we rolled into Inglewood, California, driving through a dense pea soup fog. It was a slow and exhausting drive, but finally, we found the apartment I had rented. I rented the upstairs of a two-story house belonging to a family from Maine that had retired to this warmer climate. It was a spacious place with two bedrooms, a bath and kitchenette. There was a private entrance up the stairs on the back side of the house. In the yard below was an avocado tree, which we were told to pick as desired.

The college was pretty much a straight walk of a mile or so down the street. It was all a grand adventure in an ideal setting. I started my studies in aeronautical engineering while Rod began at the airframe mechanical program nearby. As we settled into college and tech school life respectively, it was obvious that Rod was not happy. He was not comfortable in the big city. He longed for the environment he left, a small village in the desert. He descended from a long line of outdoorsmen, his father was a fur trapper from the Sangre de Christo in New Mexico.

When summer term was over, Rod returned to Cochise, Arizona and I was on my own. By then however, I had accepted the fact that his departure was the result of our different experiences and personalities and had nothing to do with our friendship. Anyway, I had already made many new friends at the college. Three in particular, stand out in my memory; Otto from Germany, "Mike" from Hungary, and Ricardo from Cuba. Each of their families had escaped from Communist regimes and immigrated to the USA. They would sometimes share their firsthand experiences when we got together, especially on our many trips to the beach after class.

I think Mike's actual name was Mihály or something close to that and his last name was totally unpronounceable, so we just gave him an American nickname. His family had recently escaped Budapest during the 1956 Russian invasion of Hungary. Likewise Ricardo's family had left Cuba during the revolution. Otto had survived WWII and the Russian takeover of Eastern Germany. Now we were all studying aerospace technology together in Southern California. I savored this camaraderie, which was the result of amazing and unique historic events.

I also joined the Pacific Rocket Society, the Society of Automotive Engineers, and the Astronomy Club. I sold my car which kept breaking down and bought a used Harley Davidson motorcycle. I ground telescope mirrors, constructed rocket engines, participated in rocket launches in the Mohave Desert and much more. It is impossible to relate all the many experiences that followed. An exceptional one however, should be mentioned.

On October 4, 1957, the Russians launched Sputnik I. Overnight, a group of aerospace corporations had constructed an optical fence to track the satellite and student members of the Pacific Rocket Society manned the telescopes in shifts to plot the orbit. It was a once-in-a-lifetime experience to be a part of that historic group. Over fifty years later, I was surprised by a glimpse of my younger self in a documentary on space exploration. There I was behind a telescope waiting for Sputnik!

By the following summer, I had run low on college savings. After discussing the situation with Mom and Dad, I decided to continue my studies at a less expensive public college in New Mexico, where I would be eligible for in-state tuition of one hundred forty dollars per semester, a small fraction of the tuition at NIT. Living expenses would also be much less.

    Little did I know that this decision would soon set in motion a series of events to completely change the direction of my life.

Me standing in front of my room 50 years later.

A New Room

Some parts of our lives are unsettling transitions. One such time occurred in 1958, the year I left the college in California and to begin another program at a university in New Mexico. It was a surreal time of great change when the familiar anchors I took for granted were all swept away. What I realized later was that creating a sense of belonging is a participatory process.

When I left home to start college in California, my family was farming near Willcox, Arizona. Returning nearly two years later, I found them living in the mountain community of Show Low. My father and mother decided to trade their share of the Willcox farm for a house and five acres in Show Low. It was a great spot nestled high in the White Mountains among the Ponderosa Pines, the exact kind of place many of us might choose to live if we could.

However, there were few opportunities to make a living there. Dad found work with the Arizona Highway Department in that district, but it was seasonal work. When the opportunity to buy farmland with water rights and an irrigation well came along Mom and Dad made the decision to sell out and move once again. Since I was present while this was happening, I was able to help with the move.

After the last of the family belongings were loaded onto large farm trailers, and we said goodbye to the house in the mountains, our little caravan slowly drove away from Show Low toward our destination near Deming, New Mexico, 250 miles away. Mom and Dad were leading the way in the front tandem while I drove the second one behind them.

It was slow going with our loaded vehicles and there were many stops along the way, but finally, late that afternoon, we arrived to a flat dusty plain of cleared land with one humble little frame house setting upon concrete blocks. It was a bleak welcome, contrasted to the idyllic setting we left behind. Every gust of breeze kicked up dust from the dry ground to welcome us. Dad had purchased a small frame house and had it moved to the land from the old mining town of Bayard near Silver City. This was to be our new family home for years to come.

That Fall and Winter, I resumed my studies at New Mexico State in Las Cruces and also helped the rest of our family to start our new life. During the week, I commuted the one hundred fifty miles round trip with Ricardo Alba, a high school classmate who was also attending the university. In between, I helped remodel the old house. It was just a bare shell. It required a septic tank, plumbing, wiring, subfloor, linoleum, caulking and insulating, painting, remodeling rooms, etc. Alternately, I helped dad with surveying the fields, harrowing, leveling, subsoiling, and plowing furrows. All this work needed to be completed in time for spring planting.

The old house had one bedroom and one tiny bathroom, so it took some creativity to make bedrooms for my sister Judy and myself. We converted the middle of the house into a makeshift bedroom/storeroom and added a bathroom to a space behind the kitchen. This left the old six foot by six foot bathroom to convert to my bedroom. It was too small for furniture, other than perhaps a chair, but I was determined to make a functioning bedroom out of it.

First, I restored the floor, the walls and painted the entire room. Next, I made a built-in bed with storage underneath, built in wall cabinets over the bed and above the door and a built-in desk on one side of the door. It became a very functional, compact bedroom. I had literally made a place of my own, one I stayed in off-and-on until I graduated from college and joined the Army.

The saying "Home is where the heart is," sums it up. I had put a share of heart into that room. Later Mom and Dad remodeled the house, and moved my room out to the farmyard where it became a tool shed. Fifty years later, I opened it's door and looked inside, it still felt more like home than many other places I've lived since that eventful year shared with my family so long ago.

The University

At New Mexico State in Las Cruces I started out as a physics major living in a dormitory. Dr. Dressel, a German physicist, was my advisor. The first semester, he placed me into a schedule of physics theory, applied physics, differential equations, chemistry, psychology, physical education and ROTC. The second semester my schedule included quantum mechanics, differential equations II, biology, English literature, economics, physical education and ROTC. I was beginning to feel less than satisfied with my program. Looking back it allowed little room for anything except study, study, and more study, and it lacked the full support of faculty and upperclassmen I had taken for granted at Northrop.

I did make some wonderful friends however. Hanging out with them started me thinking, and more importantly, feeling possibilities for life I hadn't considered before. I started out in the dorm with another physics major sharing the room. But the second semester, my roommate was a navy veteran on the GI bill, who wasn't too interested in his studies. My next roommate was an art major from Kansas City, studying on a music scholarship. I was rapidly gaining new insights into various aspects of life. It was also the beginning of the Beat Generation, Kerouac's "On The Road" was beginning to seed a great change.

The third term, I signed up for still more advanced physics and math, but I was troubled that I had done so. I felt like a deflated balloon, definitely out of enthusiasm for this path. Deep in thought, I wandered across the campus, walking through buildings I never had been in before. It was partly out of feeling aimless, and partly because it was cold and windy. Finally, I entered one of the older buildings, a rambling structure with lights on inside, which made it inviting in the twilight of the day. Wandering in, I entered a gallery of artwork. It was as interesting as a museum. From there I wandered into studio after studio, each with a variety of the different media created there. It was mesmerizing and time stood still.

I don't know how long I was in the building, but I never encountered another person, and it was totally dark outside as I started down a hall of office doors toward an exit. Near the end, there was light coming out of a partly open door and I heard a voice say, "May I help you?"

Then, as if it was someone else speaking, I heard my own hesitant reply. "...Maybe you can,...uh...wha..what does it take to major in something here...?" By this time I could see the man sitting behind the desk. He was an older fellow with grey hair wearing a tweed coat but no necktie.

"Have a seat and tell me about your background." he said.

It was well into the evening when I left the office with a file of paper work. It contained drop slips for the science curriculum I was already registered for, add slips for the new classes in fine arts, an outline of a new course of study with a plan for matriculation within a similar timeframe. Professor Paul Mannen became my new advisor replacing Professor Ralph Dressel.

Pad Sherwood

If it wasn't for my economics class being in the middle of the afternoon, I would never have discovered a way to move out of the dormitories and into a house while paying far less for rent. To begin with, Economics Class was very boring, and the lectures were linear, monotone presentations of the book chapters, exactly the recipe for an afternoon nap. To stay awake, I would doodle on my notebook paper in the middle of my attempt to make lecture notes.

A young man, about my age, sitting in the row to my left, glimpsed some of my doodles and slipped me a note to ask about them. That began a semester long conversation via notes written on scraps of paper. When it began, I could not imagine where that conversation would soon lead.

The young man was named Mike, and when he found out I lived in the dorm, he asked if I had ever thought about moving into an apartment or house. I told him that I did think about that a lot, but hadn't found anything affordable yet. He wrote me another note, which let me know he was living in a large house near downtown, which had been made into a duplex. The front 2 bedroom portion was for rent. It also had a large living room, full bath and eat-in kitchen. Further, he said if I had some friends that could share it with me it could really make it affordable. He said if we doubled up in the bedrooms or used a sofa bed in the living room it could conceivably sleep up to 5 or 6.

As I read his description, my excitement was growing. I scribbled my reply and passed it to him. "How much is the rent?" I wrote. The reply came back penciled in on my note. $50.00 a month including utilities was all it said. Wow! That was a bargain I thought. Even in 1958, that was low rent. If I could only get one more person to share the rent it would be fantastic.

I went to see it after class. It was an even better deal

than Mike described. I found out Mike was the owner and the property had been left to him by his grandparents. He lived in the rear portion of the large adobe house he had described to me, and he wanted to rent the front part. It already had utilities which he was using, so he simply included a share in the rent. Heating and cooling were not much of a cost factor in an adobe house anyway.

In addition to all this, there was plenty of furniture and appliances available in a storage building next door. The house could be furnished to any extent needed at no extra cost. It was also in an ideal location at the intersection of two almost parallel streets South of downtown Las Cruces and only a short distance from the University that Mike and I were attending. "Holy Cow!" I thought, "It would be more than foolish to pass this opportunity up."

I thanked Mike and told him I would give him an answer by tomorrow. Then I immediately went to present the idea of sharing the place to three of my best college buddies. I kind of expected maybe one of them to accept the concept, but they all thought it was a great idea. By that very evening, we had all toured the place again and all four of us became Mike's tenants, by chipping in twelve-fifty apiece for the first month.

It was an adventure moving in. After a few trips to the storage building next door, we selected two refrigerators for the kitchen, a round of beds for the bedrooms, a sofa bed for the living room, and a round of various chairs to places where they were needed. It was transformed into one of the best bachelor pads in town.

At the time we moved in, I was taking archery for one of my P.E. requirements and I needed to keep up my weekly practice time in addition to the university archery range practice done in class. I discovered that placing a hay bale target in the house, opening a couple of doors to the outside, walking across the street to the side of the canal resulted in the appropriate target distance. I could practice, but only when no one else was home, or when everyone else participated, and of course, when no car was coming. For the rest of the semester, this unusual practice turned into a regular afternoon event. My roommates and I would hold archery practice across a city street with a canal on one side and our adobe house containing the target on the opposite side. In honor of this ceremony, we named our part of the rambling adobe duplex "Pad Sherwood" and so it became known across the university and beyond.

Six Feet Under

It was the end of a typical busy day for university students. After we all returned to the duplex from class my three roommates held an impromptu jazz jam session. All three of them were musicians. Ken played trumpet, Ole played trombone, and Gus played saxophone. My only participation was by adding a few licks on bongos now and then.

After the session, we got the books out and drifted to our respective rooms and corners in an attempt catch up our homework. One evening about midnight I became hungry and looked in the refrigerator for a snack, but it was empty. So I started asking around to see if anyone knew what fast food establishment nearby might still be open. The consensus was that there was a hamburger restaurant that was open until 1 AM within walking distance.

Soon we were headed out to find a late night snack. It turned out to be a longer walk than we anticipated, we barely made it in time. The person at the counter said we could only get our orders to go this close to closing time. Soon we were carrying our treasured meals back to our place through the crisp autumn night.

We were walking fast because of hunger and also wanting semi-warm food upon return. About three-fourths of the way someone said, "We can take a short cut through the cemetery and save some time."

"Great, anything that will save time." I chimed in and headed through the shadowy gate. Suddenly, it became very dark. Clouds covered the moon completely. We stumbled across the grass and ground of the cemetery headed in the general direction we were headed before the clouds moved in. Soon we would be across and safely on the opposite side.

Suddenly, before I could react, I was falling, feet first, straight down. I landed on my feet still clutching the sack with my

hamburger, fries and shake. The next instant my momentum slammed me against a wall of dirt. I yelled, "I fell in a grave!"
I admit being somewhat panicked, in the pitch dark night one's imagination can run a bit wild. I started to imagine what could be in the grave with me. Ken lit his cigarette lighter to see where I was, and soon everyone was leaning over the edge trying to help me out. I passed up the rumpled sack containing my meal first. Then I grabbed a proffered hand and scrambled hastily up, while hearing the dirt falling that I knocked off with my shoes.

"Thanks everybody" I offered. As I dusted myself off, I added, "It's good to be back from the grave".

"You're acting pretty spunky for someone who's just been six feet under." said Gus, as we hurried on.

It turned out to be an unforgettable way to appease the midnight munchies. Never did a lukewarm, well massaged hamburger taste so good beyond the grave!

The Organ Mountains

The Organ Mountains are named after their resemblance to a church pipe organ. Standing almost nine thousand feet, the shear rock peaks are clustered together like the organ pipes they resemble. The granite peaks themselves rise a significant portion of this total above the lower slopes rimming the valley of the Rio Grande.

One Friday Autumn morning in the late 1950s, an International Harvester Travelall stopped on primitive gravel road that wound through the high plateau and mountain foothills. Out climbed our group, four intrepid university students, each with packs of camping gear. This strategic bend in the road near the base of the Organ Mountains was positioned under the highest peaks looming above. After thanking the driver and saying, "See you here Sunday evening," we all shouldered our packs and started to wind our way up the mountain slopes. Our assault on the peaks began that day. By late that first afternoon, our party had carried our gear up the mountains several thousand feet to a promising spot high on the steep slopes. A campsite was chosen as near the rise of the stone monoliths of the peak formations as possible. There were very few places for bedrolls amid the rockslides and cactus, but just enough space was found, cleared and rearranged by moving some rocks and cactus. Plenty of dead cholla was gathered for a campfire, while being careful to avoid the myriad of fur-like spines on the dry "skin" still clinging to the branches and also fallen around them. One careless touch could inflict serious pain plus hours of finding and pulling the spines out.

Three of us had some basic experience climbing around in the western mountain ranges, but the fourth did not. Jim grew up in Nashville, Tennessee, and this was the first time he ever had been in such inhospitable terrain. So far though, he was doing as well as the rest of us. We were all in our late teens and early twenties, in the prime of our lives. This adventure was just the sort of thing we loved to do.

By evening, we had started a roaring campfire to cut the chill. We kept it going until it was time to get some rest for the climb the next day. Sleep was fitful at best perched in sleeping bags on thin pads amid the uneven rocks. Dawn found the group sipping coffee and making breakfast. Then the bedrolls, spare canteens, and food were packed away while daypacks were prepared with just enough supplies for the strenuous one-day climb.

We set off toward the base of the peaks nearby scouting out possible routes to the top. This was a freestyle climb, or scramble. We had no climbing gear other than our hands and booted feet. Any way up was possible as long as it had sufficient hand and toe holds and crevasses. Often we would try climbing in one direction only to come to a spot that did not seem passable. When that happened the lead climber would call out the situation and the party would tediously back down, one by one to a spot that would allow a change of direction.

Mid-morning, we decided to split into two teams of two people in order to double our efforts in trying routes up different faces of the peaks. We planned to meet again later at the same place to share our findings. Plan B was to rendezvous at the base camp at the end of the day.

Gus and I set off in one direction, Jim and Ken in another. We quickly lost sight of the other pair and focused on our chosen route up. Scrambling from handhold to handhold we made good progress, stopping occasionally to rest and reconsider the possibilities ahead. By early afternoon Gus and I were on the peak, euphoric with the panoramic views. We stayed up there, yelling out our success in the hope our companions, wherever they were, could hear us. Then we sat down on the great rock of the peak to rest and shared some water and jerky prior to our descent. After resting we discussed possible routes downward that might make it easier going down than retracing our route up.

A promising new possibility was chosen, and we began picking our way down another face of the Peak. It was past mid afternoon by that time and we needed to get back to base camp before dark. I was leading the descent and saw a ledge about ten feet below, which seemed to offer a similar connection to something beneath it. Making a quick decision, I slid my body down to the last handhold and let go. A moment later, I landed on the ledge. It didn't take long to realize I had made a very bad decision. After looking around the narrow ledge, It became clear there was no connection to anything lower. It cut back to overhang a drop below, I guessed 150 feet to the next place to stand.
As I was taking all this in, I heard Gus say, "How does it look down there? Should I come down too?"

"No, stay where you are! There is no way down from

here." I hollered. It was quiet for a moment as our words echoed down the cliffs.

I tried to jump up to reach a possible handhold above, only to slide down the rock face each time. Finally, I said to Gus, "Maybe you can help me out of here."

"How?" pondered Gus, "I don't have any rope, do you?"

"No, I never climb with rope, but I sure could use some now," I regretfully mused, then added, "Let me think and look around a little."

To which Gus replied, "Don't think too long, the sun is going lower."

In my mind I was picturing the way I held on to things before I let go to slide down to where I was.

Then I described this to Gus, "There is a scrawny little branch a juniper maybe, in a crack in the rock face on the right, a foot or so down to the left is a good hand hold in the rock face, but you can't see it until you are holding on to the branch going down. If you hang on to these two things, maybe I can jump up far enough to reach your boot."

There was silence as Gus pondered this crazy plan. Then as I was actually thinking it would be saner and safer for him just to go get help, he blurted out, " Oh what the Hell, let's try it!"

I heard the cussing and grunting above as Gus found the juniper and then the rock face to grip. Then, I saw a boot sole and heel dangling above me.

"Hold on for both of us!" I said as I jumped as high as I could. My fingers caught the top of Gus's boot and I momentarily hung there, and then pulled up far enough to grab with two hands then grab some pants legs and belt and I scrambled up over Gus to the perch above him, pushing off his shoulders to safety. Then as I found more handholds I returned the favor as Gus scrambled back up beside me.

Exhausted, we panted together in silence and then I said,

"Thanks, you saved me, you son of a gun!"

"You're welcome, anything to help a buddy," he replied.

We made it back to base camp to find the others waiting. They told us that they had been unsuccessful in getting all the way up and had finally turned around late in the afternoon.

Right then, Jim got up to find more cholla for the fire, walking out to the edge of the rock slide. Then as the rest of us watched in horror, the rocks started moving, Jim's weight triggered a rock slide and down he went over the edge on top of the tumbling rocks.

We all scrambled after him, disregarding the consequences. By then the slide had stabilized enough to stay put as we reached him, simultaneously trying to help him up. It was then we saw the true picture. Not only was Jim bruised and shaken, but he was covered with cholla spines all over! It was the worst possible outcome except for being buried under rocks.

We helped him back up the short distance to camp and tried to remove as many thorns as possible so he could at least sit down. There was no way we could achieve the goal however. Removing the larger visible spines was only part of the problem. Hundreds of tiny spines were still imbedded in his skin. Barely visible in bright daylight, they were impossible to see in the fading twilight we were enveloped in.

Jim was beyond miserable as we took turns, far into the night, continuing to remove spines that could be discovered by flickering firelight, dim flashlight and touch. He moaned and groaned stoically as we went about our grim task, letting out a scream now and then as we jerked hooked cactus spines from his swollen, bleeding skin.

Finally exhausted, we covered Jim by the fire and left him in his misery for a few hours while the rest of us grabbed a little fitful sleep. At dawn, we packed up and started a slow descent. At least Jim didn't have spines on his feet, which were still in his boots. It was hard to support him without inflicting more pain, but we did the best we could. Sharing the support of Jim and the extra gear made the descent very slow.

At last we arrived at the designated pick-up spot. After waiting for a hour or so, we saw the telltale dust trail from the road below and grew more euphoric as the Travelall came into view. Jim was propped in, gear stowed and we all headed for the emergency room, where he could receive needed medical attention. So ended our adventure of scaling the Organ Mountains. The last I heard, Jim had healed, and was safely back in Nashville where he intended to stay.

The Volcano

On two separate occasions in my life, I worked inside volcanoes. The first experience was for a few days, the second would be for over a year. The first time began when out of the blue my cousin Jerry called me on the old rotary phone at my parents home saying, "I have a Summer job with the Museum of New Mexico working in the boot heel down past Animas. They need another hand if you're interested."

"Doing what?" I asked.

"Excavating in a cave the archeologists and anthropologists are studying in the Alamo Hueco Mountains. It is actually a volcano vent, not a regular cave," he explained.

"How long ago did this volcano erupt?" I asked.

"You can relax, its dormant," Jerry went on, "It last erupted thousands of years ago. Heck, the stuff they are finding in it is all prehistoric."

"Count me in," I said, not knowing that young adults, like myself, were easily placated with mentions of volcanic dormancy. They haven't yet realized there is really no such thing as a dormant volcano. Volcanos simply follow a totally different time scale than humans.

The camp, according to Jerry, was located somewhere above a certain arroyo where a ranchers' windmill and water tank were located near the base of some mountains. Since the others would already be there, I would have to find a way to the camp myself. Jerry continued filling me in on all the details including how the scientist leading the expedition was married to the daughter of our family Doctor.

I managed to persuade my dad to drive me the seventy-five miles from the family farm to the camp. I packed my bedroll, enough clothes and sundries for the expedition and off we went. However, by the time we got to Diamond A Ranch country it was dark. We drove around looking for any light that might reveal the camp, but with no luck.

Finally, I said to Dad, "Just let me out, I'm pretty sure this is the same arroyo and I'll just follow it up toward the mountains in the morning daylight."

It was a dry, cloudless sky with the Milky Way sparkling all across it, so I simply laid my bedroll down on arroyo sand and went to sleep. I woke up the next morning to the cooing of a pair of doves. When I finished rolling up and tying my sleeping bag, I headed up the arroyo. After walking for about twenty minutes, I went up a sand dune between two bushy mesquites and walked right into the muzzle of a twelve-gauge, double barrel shotgun. "Whoa!" I exclaimed, stopping right where I was, and dropping my bedroll.

"Sorry, you scared the shit out of me sneak'n in like that." said the man lowering the shotgun.

"I wasn't trying to sneak. I'm looking for the State Museum Camp." I said.

"Well you found it. I'm cooking breakfast. How about some coffee?" By then he had put down the shotgun and picked up a large chuck wagon style coffee pot off of a Coleman kerosene stove. My timing was perfect. Soon I found my cousin Jerry, met the rest of the crew and had some breakfast.

The first thing we did after breakfast was load all the gear up into a vehicle and head up a couple of ruts which served as a road toward the base of a slope. There the digging gear was unloaded and taken piece by piece, several hundred feet up the slope to a small cave-like entrance in the base of the cliff.

"Why isn't the gear just left up there until the excavation is finished?" I asked.

"Because, we never know when we will be finished. We keep on until the scientists are satisfied we have excavated everything of interest the site may contain," was the reply.

I was told the initiation rite for a new hired hand was to be the first to go in the vent. Sure enough, it happened.

"You will be the first one to start bringing in gear," the leader instructed me. I was told how to slither into the vent opening on my back pulling the rope in with me. Once in, I was to light my headlamp, pull the rope to signal those outside, who would then tie on a collapsed wheelbarrow filled with shovels, trowels and supplies. Upon their signal back, I was to pull it into the cave like a sled. After that, it was simply waiting to assist the others. When everyone made it into the vent, gear could be assembled for the day's work.

In the gloom my headlamp illuminated the interior of the volcano vent revealing the excavation pit and the passage continuing into the inky darkness. It was kind of spooky being alone in there, even if it was only temporary. You couldn't help but think just how very little change in the narrow tunnel would prevent slithering in or out. Having the new guy go in first was a perfect way to see if he was going to be able to handle the job.

One by one I was joined by the others, which was reassuring. We assembled the wheelbarrows, put on our respirators and headlamps, and set to work. Our job was to dig the pit down one foot at a time, and to sift each shovelful of compressed bat guano for possible artifacts. The large square sifters were made of a 2x4 frames with wire mesh attached to the bottom. After filling a wheelbarrow with sifted leavings the waste was pushed back into the bowels of the volcano until the horizontal vent shaft we were working in met the throat of the volcano. There, we eased up to the edge and dumped the load down. One could hear it raining down long enough to guess it was a long way down to a resting place. This was quite a dramatic volcano anatomy lesson to say the least. I learned that any small, pleasant looking, mountain in your neighborhood may be hiding some deep, dark secrets that it may reveal at any given moment.

I found out the vent floor we were excavating was composed of thousands of years of bat guano deposits. It was also pointed out to me that breathing the air and dust in there could be very hazardous, so therefore we wore goggled respirators. It also helped to button, zipper, tie and lace everything we wore to the max. That didn't keep out all of it, but it did cut down on the interior guano deposits we all accumulated during the days work.

The highlight of the working day for us cave workers came after we pulled the equipment out of the vent, lifted it back down the mountainside, stowed it away and headed for the water tank under the windmill. There, we all striped into our birthday suits and dove into the cold water to wash away the guano de jour. Also we rinsed the clothes we wore that day and hung them to dry so they could serve us again later.

For those of us doing the excavating, it was pretty exiting to find a pre-Columbian artifact or a bone from a prehistoric creature. I was curious to learn what the scientific team thought about these objects. Among the finds during this expedition was a rabbit net made of human hair, which unrolled was over three hundred feet long. Among the other artifacts were a quiver full of flint tipped arrows, pairs of sandals, saber tooth bones and prehistoric bison bones. All this was over the top excitement for me, but totally humdrum for the scientists. It seems late prehistoric human artifacts and early prehistoric beasts were not exciting for them, but almost too ordinary. I found out what they were really searching for. What they really hoped to discover was evidence of early prehistoric man in North America.

Periodically, some of the scientific leaders would inform the rest of the crew that they were taking the four wheel drive I.H. Travelall on the long drive back to town for supplies. Supplies were very important to the expedition, but the rest of us knew the underlying reason for these trips were actually to visit the Silver Dollar Saloon and drown their sorrows over such sorry luck.

www.ingramcontent.com/pod-product-compliance
Lightning Source LLC
Chambersburg PA
CBHW020616300426
44113CB00007B/662